"Essayist and critic Brian Dillon is in thrall to sentences. For a quarter
he tells us in his marvelous new book, he has been collecting them.... The product of decades of close reading, *Suppose a Sentence* is eclectic yet tightly shaped....
The best and certainly most beautiful piece in the book is on Roland Barthes,
'the patron saint of my sentences' without whom 'I would never have written a
word.' It is easy to understand what Mr. Dillon means when he speaks of Barthes,
one of whose books is called *A Lover's Discourse*, as 'the most seductive writer
I know,' for Mr. Dillon's own book is a record of successive enrapturings."
—John Banville, *The Wall Street Journal*

"Dillon, with his *Suppose a Sentence*, a collection of reflections on the nature of
the sentence, made me wonder why any of the rest of us bother trying to write
non-fiction."
—Ian Sansom, *The Times Literary Supplement*

"These chronologically arranged picks from the 17th century to today are the
'few that shine more brightly and for the moment compose a pattern.' The author
plumbs biography, autobiography, and history to add context and background,
with particular attention to each author's literary style.... A learned, spirited
foray into what makes a sentence tick."
—*Kirkus Reviews*

"The book has a lot of what I can only call pleasure—of the kind that I imagine
athletes or dancers experience when they are doing what they do, which is then
communicated to those watching them do it. I share with Dillon some misgivings
about general theories and overarching ideas, but in thinking about the writing
I enjoy most, this quality feels like the one constant: that the author takes some
pleasure in using these muscles and finding them capable of what they are asked.
That delight is evident both in the sentences Dillon looks at and in those he
writes himself."
—Hasan Altaf, *The Paris Review*

"Reducing great writers and works to a single sentence is a provocative act, but
one that in an age of 280-character opinions does not feel inappropriate. Used
as we are to monosyllabic messaging and governance by tweet, it is an important
reminder of the potential beauty, rather than mere convenience, that can be conjured in concision.... *Suppose a Sentence* is an absorbing defense of literary originality and interpretation, inviting us not just to take words as they first appear
but to let them abstract themselves before our very eyes."
—Chris Allnutt, *Financial Times*

"I loved *Suppose a Sentence* by Brian Dillon. It's pleasingly nerdy: a collection of short essays, each on a single sentence, each mixing close reading, biography and the occasional dazzling flash of insight into the pure pleasure of reading and why we bother to do it at all."

—Daniel Swift, *The Spectator*

"Dillon's writing plays an exquisite critical sensibility against an exuberant celebratory impulse. He homes in on particular formal decisions (why is this comma here rather than there) and he makes it clear why he loves the sentences he does.... Dillon, like all good critics, refuses the distinction between hermeneutics and erotics. He shows how pleasurable sentences can be, and he does so through supple, sophisticated interpretation."

—Anthony Domestico, *Commonweal*

"Ultimately, this is a book about love...On the frequent occasions that Dillon is overtaken by enthusiasm for the prose machinery...he resembles a professor of anatomy falling into a cadaver in his enthusiasm...This is no bad thing."

—*ArtReview*

"Deeply engaging critical work...entertaining and insightful...Dillon's great achievement has been to gather the voices of his subjects into a single room, succinctly and effectively portraying the echo chamber in which all literary creation takes place."

—Kit Maude, *The Coachella Review*

"Brian Dillon is one of the true treasures of contemporary literature. *Suppose a Sentence* is an inspired celebration of the sentence as a self-sufficient artform, and reading it has reinvigorated my sense of the possibilities of writing itself."

—Mark O'Connell

"Brian Dillon has a way with and among ideas, rather an unusual one. His acute noticing supposes, as he says along with Gertrude Stein, a singular sentence in some text of these wildly differing authors, and then expands upon that notice, moving us around within and without the very particular wording to the everything else around. He dives in for some detail(s) of each called-upon part of a whole, surprising us and himself by his swerves and metaswerves, offering them delightedly up to a joint self-awareness in the reading. Very close-up and personal, the style wrapping around itself, like the ouroboros, this animal waiting to be found."

—Mary Ann Caws

"Reading Brian Dillon's brilliant book, I was repeatedly struck—because each one of the book's short sections is a wholly captivating demonstration of this fact—that a sentence, just a single sentence, can hold and release an event. 'Close reading,' in Dillon's hands, starts to look like a form of 'close living': a life-practice that makes an everyday value out of paying serious, open-minded attention, especially to what is hard to understand."

—Kate Briggs

Suppose a Sentence

BRIAN DILLON

nyrb **New York Review Books** New York

This is a New York Review Book

published by The New York Review of Books

435 Hudson Street, New York, NY 10014

www.nyrb.com

Library of Congress Cataloging-in-Publication Data
Names: Dillon, Brian, 1969– author.
Title: Suppose a sentence / Brian Dillon.
Description: New York City: New York Review Books, 2020.
Identifiers: LCCN 2020011251 (print) | LCCN 2020011252 (ebook) |
   ISBN 9781681375243 (paperback) | ISBN 9781681375250 (ebook)
Subjects: LCSH: Literary style. | English language—Rhetoric. | English
   language—Sentences. | Creation (Literary, artistic, etc.)
Classification: LCC PN203.D55 2020 (print) | LCC PN203 (ebook) |
   DDC 808/.042—dc23
LC record available at https://lccn.loc.gov/2020011251
LC ebook record available at https://lccn.loc.gov/2020011252

ISBN 978-1-68137-524-3
Available as an electronic book; ISBN 978-1-68137-525-0

Printed in the United States of America on acid-free paper.

10 9 8 7 6 5 4 3 2

For Emily LaBarge

"Unless for some perverts the sentence is a *body*?"
—ROLAND BARTHES, *The Pleasure of the Text* (1973)

"You can never know enough, never work enough, never use the infinitives and participles oddly enough, never impede the movement harshly enough, never leave the mind quickly enough."
—ANNE CARSON, *Short Talks* (1992)

Contents

Sensibility as Structure 13

What, Gone Without a Word? (*William Shakespeare*). . . 24

Fair Hopes of Ending All (*John Donne*) 26

O Altitudo (*Sir Thomas Browne*) 33

Daguerreotype, &c. (*Thomas De Quincey*). 37

The Exaltation of Lucy Snowe (*Charlotte Brontë*) 50

A History of the Lights and Shadows (*George Eliot*) 56

Traditions of Air (*John Ruskin*) 64

Suppose a Sentence (*Gertrude Stein*) 78

How How How What What What How—When
    (*Virginia Woolf*). 81

All Kinds of Obscure Tensions (*Samuel Beckett*) 88

(Small Pictures 1915–1940) (*Frank O'Hara*) 100

Splinters of Actuality (*Elizabeth Bowen*) 103

Obeying the Form of the Curve (*James Baldwin*) 108

The Grand Illusion (*Joan Didion*) 116

A Tour of the Monuments (*Robert Smithson*) 131

It Is Only a Paper Dagger (*Maeve Brennan*) 136

To Eat Is Not to Respect a Menu (*Roland Barthes*) 140

Albeit Succoured by a Cult (*Whitney Balliett*) 150

The Cunning of Destruction (*Elizabeth Hardwick*) 155

Suite Vénitienne (*Susan Sontag*) 163

A Ritual Feat (*Annie Dillard*) 171

Broken Tongue (*Theresa Hak Kyung Cha*) 177

Saving Imprecision (*Janet Malcolm*) 182

Surprised His Shoes (*Fleur Jaeggy*) 190

Before She Solidified (*Hilary Mantel*) 198

Gusto Notwithstanding (*Claire-Louise Bennett*) 207

Or Some Not-Stupid Sentences (*Anne Carson*) 217

Like How If (*Anne Boyer*) 219

Readings 223

Acknowledgments 227

Sensibility as Structure

OR MAYBE A SHORT SENTENCE after all, a fragment in fact, a simple cry, of pain or pleasure, or succession of same, of the same cries that is, compounded, and spoken at the last, *in extremis*, or another sort of beast entirely, whose unmeaning cry is just an overture, before the sentence sets in distinguished motion its several parallel clauses, as though it were a creature with at least four legs ("Every sentence was once an animal," says Emerson), so slowly but deliberately intent on its progress, so stately in its procession, so lavish in attention to the world it passes through, so exacting in the concentration it demands in turn, that—what?—here already the sentence swerves, and although you are sure you've caught the sense the shape has begun to elude you, as if the animal in question were squirming or shaking itself loose of your grip, or turning to bite you and then take off, against all entreaties, into a mist of metaphor, where you must follow, closing the gate of this punctuation mark behind you; and on the other side everything is both less certain and suddenly, swimmingly, closer at hand: the sentence stops and looks around and starts comparing itself to the action of a drug, to the light-sucking lens of a camera or the slow apparition of an image (let's say a face) on photographic paper, to festive decorations enchained about a church, or a storm speeding across the lake towards the place where its writer is sitting, or, or, or the sentence, which considers itself very modern, has grown tired of such figural adventures, not to speak of the antiquary's accumulation of clauses and subclauses, so that you start to notice, start to notice certain acts of repetition (Repetition. But also. Interruption.) that give the sentence a faceted, crystalline quality it will always ever after possess, whether it wants to talk about sickness and health, about the sunlight outside Rome, a New York afternoon, a white boy who wants to be black, or the disappearing sun in daytime, even if it is short, even if it is long, even (especially) if it still aspires to its old elegance, the lofty periods, the plush vocabulary, on which subject, by the way, the sentence has been taking notes—a sample from the archive: *slumgullion, mandrelled, greaved, eidetic, soricine, macula, flimmering, glop, exorb, chthonic, brumous, moil, ort, flygolding, chlamys*—and keeping tabs, in case these riches come in useful, because who can say what the sentence will need or want in the future, what expansions or contractions it may endure or enjoy, what knowledge need to muster and deploy, whose speech to steal and celebrate, where to be heard the rhythms it needs to live, to live and let slip your overly attentive attention, interesting itself in things and bodies and abstractions that you no longer recognize and whose names and outlines you will have to entrust to the slippery sentence itself, which it turns out knows more than you do, knows when to seize on and worry the world and when to let go, as it's doing now, and go skittering away from you (its maker not its keeper), beating the bounds of its invisible domain.

For about twenty-five years I have been copying sentences into the back pages of whatever notebook I happen to be using, using mostly for other purposes. The brand, style and quality of these notebooks has changed a few times, but not their dimensions, or not much: they are all more or less A5, paperback-sized, at home in the hand or on the desk. Of course there are sentences elsewhere in these books: even the briefest, most telegraphic, verbless note is a sentence of sorts. And then there are the quotations and paraphrases from books, descriptions of people and places and things, as well as rough drafts of sentences later to be properly written, or not written. But the end-of-notebook sentences are different, even if some of them come from books I'm reviewing and so on. Unconnected to duty or deadlines, to *projects* per se, they compose a parallel timeline—of what?

I suppose the word is: *affinity*. On the bookshelves behind me as I'm writing now, there are forty-five of those notebooks, a phalanx of black spines interrupted by the occasional red or blue, and even one or two spiral bindings. One day, I might track down others, which are lost among books and papers, and put the whole lot in chronological order. For now, choose a notebook from the shelves at random, and who knows what sliver of time will come with it, or what sentences. Here are some examples from a notebook I was using late in 2009. Walter Benjamin: "Our life, it can be said, is a muscle strong enough to contract the whole of historical time." Walter Pater: "In aesthetic criticism the first step towards seeing one's object as it really is, is to know one's own impression as it really is." (This one, it turns out, is extracted from a longer sentence in *The Renaissance*.) Tim Robinson: "Of course the justness of a word sometimes resides in the precise degree of discomfort it inflicts." Robinson again: "All you can feel is the cold, flowing down from the pulseless heart of the icefield." D. H. Lawrence: "And my diamond might be coal or soot, and my theme is carbon." Finally, a fragment from a sentence, unattributed: "had fitted, as the air for human breath, so the clouds...." (It is by John Ruskin.) Apart from the dismaying maleness of this selection, and some progress away from the abstractions of history and aesthetics towards the particulars of geology and weather, I notice something else. The first three sentences seem the sort of thing I might have saved for subsequent quotation; they sound self-assured, prodding their general points home. Between the two sentences from Robinson—an incomparable essayist on earth and atmosphere—everything changes. What did I think I was seeing in these other sentences? Or hearing, or hoping to emulate? With the first three, it's obvious: an epigrammatic snap, some truth at odds with received wisdom, a relevance to writing, a degree of portability: as a critic, I can imagine insinuating any one of them into an essay or review. Maybe not without a little pomp and satisfaction. But the others? How to say, because this must be the word, what I *love* there?

Some of the twenty-seven sentences this book is about are derived from those notebook pages; out of a teeming sky of inscriptions, these are the few that shine more brightly and for the moment compose a pattern. But constellations are accidents of our limited vantage point, and this one could easily vanish, in fact has already folded into the larger design (if that is what it is) of all the sentences I found, or found again, once I realized I was writing a book about sentences. *About* may not be the right word—better *towards* or *among*. I knew at once that I had no general theory of the sentence, no prescriptive attitude towards the sentence, nor aspired to write its history. If I must (and I felt I must) write about my relationship with sentences, I would have to follow my instinct for the particular. Thus twenty-seven essays of varied lengths—I was aiming for twenty-five, and overshot—each of which looks at, or wanders away from, a single sentence.

The piece on Elizabeth Hardwick came first, Hardwick who believed (as Darryl Pinckney put it) that "sensibility is structure." I wondered if it was enough to extract a sentence and hope something would ramify from there, like a crystal. When I started, I had not yet read Roland Barthes's essay about seven sentences in Flaubert: "We must never forget in our commentaries and digressions that our point of departure is the shattering obviousness of an object of language that we have cut from its discursive artifice, its ideological artificiality." I was attracted to this image of reading as cutting, as if the critic's eye were akin to the collagist's scalpel. I began to think of this book as having something in common with photomontage, an art of excision and juxtaposition. Or the single sentence as a Duchampian readymade, an object (coat rack, urinal, snow shovel) plucked from its context and made enigmatic, if not abstract. What if my writing about these sentences succeeded only in making them more opaque?

I had other models in mind too. I've always relished the invitation, which has sometimes come my way, to write about a single thing: one poem, one work of art, one image, best of all one photograph—a film still, for example. (Susan Sontag: "A photograph could also be described as a quotation, which makes a book of photographs like a book of quotations.") At the art and culture quarterly *Cabinet*, where I've been a contributing editor for years, there's a tradition of asking writers to compose a response to an artefact of the magazine's choosing. It might be a colour, or a found object the editors will provide but refuse to identify. (Sometimes even the editors have not recognized the thing.) The exercise or constraint encourages, or so one hopes, an intensified attention, though the extreme of concentration may also take the writer far away from the thing itself. It's a perilous writerly challenge, always on the verge of preciousness, treating its object as a talisman or curiosity. The best respondents embrace the delirium of the experiment, such as the poet Wayne Koestenbaum, whose short book *Notes on Glaze*—eighteen investigations of eighteen photographs—has been frequently on my mind. Koestenbaum, who writes elsewhere: "We commit a cruelty against existence if we do not interpret it to death."

Found objects—but found by whom? Could I write a book about sentences that were chosen by other people? I liked the idea but baulked at the practice. What if I hated the sentence, or its writer? Of course I could ask for the texts to be anonymized, like undergraduate essays, or like the gobbets of poetry in I. A. Richard's famous 1920s experiment in practical criticism. But then I would try to guess, which is boring, or be tempted to google, which is despicable. No, I would have to

19

choose the sentences myself, and accept the limitations of my knowledge and taste, the dimensions of my prejudice.

I allowed myself some rules, and imposed certain freedoms. For instance, if I was sufficiently attracted to a sentence that I copied it out in the new notebook I had reserved for this project, or transferred it from an old one, there was no going back. I had to write about *that* sentence, and not choose another from the same work or by the same author, let alone drop both from the list. This meant that *working on my book* referred most of the time to a frenzy of hesitation. I broke the rule only once—*au revoir*, Francis Ponge—but there are writers whose names appear in the notebook, with no sentence attached, and who later dropped out, because I lost interest, or could not find the right sentence or, shamefully, in at least one case, found I was not up to the task. Some of these losses would have been unthinkable to me when I started. To my surprise, there are no sentences here from Robert Burton, Edgar Allan Poe, Herman Melville, James Joyce, W. G. Sebald or Lydia Davis. No Emily Dickinson, no T. S. Eliot, no John Ashbery (I have neglected, but not completely, the sentence in poetry). No Proust—no Proust! Also no aphorisms or epigrams, no one-liners such as you'd find, funny or profound, in La Rochefoucauld, Oscar Wilde or E. M. Cioran. I had written too much about those well-formed philosophical fragments before, and they were too self-contained, too full of themselves, for my purposes here. I wanted sentences that would open under my gaze, not preserve or project their perfection.

One more thing this book would not do, at least directly: tell you how to write a great sentence. I have nothing against works that advise on the composition of good prose, and some of these have proved invaluable: books by Virginia Tufte, Stanley Fish and Joe Moran. Best of all: Lydia Davis's lectures on her own perfectionist notebook-keeping. But my book is not a *how to*. Still less a *how not to*, because I do have an allergy to polemics against bad writing, which are usually scolding and conservative, tending to dull defences of the "plain style," and droning on about the perils of "jargon," all the while deaf to their own obnoxious and excluding conventions. There will be no mention (apart from this one) of George Orwell's "Politics and the English Language" in this book, no diatribes against "foreign words and expressions." They are all foreign, waiting to be found.

Not this, not that—the truth is I wanted to write a book that was all positives, all pleasure, only about good things. Beautiful sentences, Gass wrote, are "rare as eclipses." I went chasing eclipses: those moments of reading when the light changes, some darker lustre takes over, things (words) seem suddenly obscure, even in the simplest sentence, and you find you have to look twice, more than twice. (In some cases I'm lagging as a reader behind translators who have been there before me, even interpreted a sentence that I cannot, remaking it; I've tried to acknowledge their writerly presence.) In 1853, the poet and critic Matthew Arnold proposed what he called literary "touchstones," those privileged moments that constitute the best of what has been thought and written, against which the relative worth of other works can be assessed. For good reasons, this is no longer a reputable way to think about literature: the texture of flux and design disappearing in the preservation of mere relics. So, not a treasury, then—something closer, I hope, to a kind of commonplace book, product of haphazard notation, ad hoc noticing.

Except, of course, it is not that: the raw notebook would be indecipherable, self-involved. And while I very much like the idea of a book made only of quotations, a *cento* without glosses, notes or scholium, not even Benjamin, who aspired to something of the sort in his *Arcades Project*, could refrain from commentary and give himself up completely to the dialectic dance of fragments. In each of the twenty-seven pieces that follow, I've tried to describe the affinity I feel for the individual sentence, perhaps also for the work it came from and the writer who composed it, but without my figuring in advance how much analysis, how much context, how much rapture or digression I would include. I wrote, as it were, with my nose to the page, wrote for the first time in my life without a plan of the whole in mind, wrote from one fragment to the next, feeling for the route that affinity might take me. As for thematic connections, all I will say is that a remarkable number seem to be about death and disappearance.

A word about extent and structure. The length of an essay does not say anything about the sentence which is its subject or starting point. In fact, there are sentences here, both celebrated and obscure, to which I wish I could have responded only with a single perfect sentence of my own. The book is organized chronologically, according to the dates of the sentences' first publication. Any other design, except perhaps an alphabetical one, seemed to work against the residual logic of the notebook, and against my hope that affinities—of tone, rhythm, grammar, word choice, architecture, worldview, argument, interests, personality, *style* in all its senses—would emerge in time, as the sentences asserted their material, immaterial presence and worked the miracle of their spectral persistence.

London, April 2020

What, Gone Without a Word?

"O, o, o, o."

—WILLIAM SHAKESPEARE

IN SHAKESPEARE, last words are rarely the last. "O, I die, Horatio," Hamlet declares about fifty lines from the end of the play that bears his name, and six lines before his own finish. His actual end follows, famously: "—the rest is silence." Not quite, or not always. There are three variant texts of *Hamlet*, and in at least one the Dane dies differently: "—the rest is silence. O, o, o, o." What are they telling us, these four diminishing "O"s? (Or is it five? The full stop, you might say, is the last and smallest circle.) "O" is everywhere in Shakespeare, as proclamation and sometimes as oral or typographic pun: "this little O, the earth"—which might also be the Globe theatre. Scholars say that Othello's "O! O! O!," uttered after he has murdered Desdemona, is a single roar of guilt and horror, not three discrete cries. Nearing the end of his life, Lear also cries

"O, O, O, O!" Lady Macbeth's "O, o, o" is heard by her doctor as a series of "sighs." And Hamlet's "O, o, o, o"? It is surely nothing more or less than the vocal expression, precisely, of silence. "O" is the tragic apotheosis of zero.

Fair Hopes of Ending All

"Wee have a *winding sheete* in our Mothers wombe, which growes with us from our conception, and wee come into the world, wound up in that winding sheet, for wee come to *seeke a grave*; And as prisoners discharg'd of actions may lye for fees; so when the *wombe* hath discharg'd us, yet we are bound to it by *cordes* of flesh, by such a *string* as that wee cannot goe thence, nor stay there."

—JOHN DONNE

THE POET AND PREACHER John Donne died from stomach cancer in the spring of 1631. He had likely been sick for a year, but continued in his office of dean at St Paul's Cathedral, where his weekly sermons were admired for their erudition, piety, and extremes of metaphorical invention. When illness made him quit the capital for his daughter's house in Essex, rumours arose that Donne was already dead, or was feigning his distemper. Gathering his strength, he returned to London in March, quite sensible of his hourly decline but resolved to deliver a last sermon, at the palace of Whitehall before King Charles I and his court. As Donne's first biographer Izaak Walton tells us, the poet's friends were appalled at his appearance—he had left about him "but so much flesh as did only cover his bones"—and they tried to dissuade him from his homiletic duty. When he rose as appointed on the first day of Lent and in a hollow voice began to speak of dissolution, decay, and the life to come, it seemed to them that he had composed his own funeral oration.

Such was Donne's devout insouciance in the face of death that in the days before he spoke the sermon, and in it this astonishing sentence, he contrived a visual counterpart, his own ghastly monument. He summoned a painter to his sickroom, who found the learned dean shrouded head to foot, his eyes closed and limbs arranged as if already in the grave. Donne had the resulting portrait set by his bedside so he could look upon it in his last days—as the critic Frank Kermode put it, the dying man seemed possessed of an "almost histrionic composure." It was on this picture (now lost) that the sculptor Nicholas Stone based the monument to Donne that still stands in St Paul's. An engraving from the same source formed the frontispiece to the final sermon when it was published in 1632: here is the ailing divine embarked on his ultimate spiritual migration, oblivious to the world of flesh even as he makes us stare at its grisly remnant.

In print, the sermon is called "Deaths Duell," though Donne never titled his sermons: nothing came before the biblical quotation that gave each one its subject and its structure. In this case the lesson is from Psalm 68, verse 20: "And unto God the Lord belong the issues of death." As was sermonic convention, Donne approaches this ambiguous line via an explicit tripartite plan. His task as preacher is, first, closely to read this text for its diverse meanings; second, to set it in the context of biblical and theological authority; third, to lay out nakedly, in a kind of moral anatomy, the lessons and models that may be taken away. "Deaths Duell" begins with another triad: a somewhat distracting architectural conceit by which Donne thinks of the psalmic text as a building, with foundations, buttresses, and joints or "contignations." But we are soon amid the fundamental truths of the text, of which there are also three. "And unto God the Lord belong the issues of death" means: He will deliver us *from* death, to eternal life; *in* death, because he will save us from undue suffering; and *by* death, for this trial is necessary to attain our reward.

So far so schematic, so theologically and rhetorically conventional. But "Deaths Duell" is also a cabinet of baroque horrors, a repository of gruesome images cast in sentences that are themselves errant or deformed. In spite of Donne's insistence on our deliverance, and his own, into eternal life, it seems at the same time that death never ends, that it reigns either side of the actual event of our leave-taking. The world, writes Donne, "is but an *universal church-yard*, but our *common grave*; and the life and motion that the greatest persons have in it, is but as the shaking of buried bodies in their graves, by an *earth-*

quake." So too, one might say, the text of his sermon itself, which is planted everywhere with corpses, some of which are in disguise as living persons. There is, of course, the noisome reality of the grave, and our being gnawed away by worms. But the most pristine picture of health is shadowed by death: even in youth, even in our infancy, even in the womb, we are already dying.

The deliciously dismal effect of all this unceasing decease is partly a matter of Donne's prose style. He wrote at a time when—better to say, he quickened the process whereby—in English the orotund Ciceronian period, a balanced type of sentence made of hierarchical clauses, complexly deferring its dying fall (or alternatively: its *o altitudo!*), was being shaken loose by a less formal, Senecan, model—a sentence onto the end of which one could dash new clauses, carelessly. Donne could do Ciceronian, for sure: in his 160 surviving sermons, there are many exquisitely ordered examples. In "Deaths Duell," he even deploys a neatly balanced sentence to tell us that life and death conspire to produce, precisely, a circular Ciceronian period: "As the first part of a sentence peeces wel with the last, and never respects, never hearkens after the *parenthesis* that comes betweene, so doth a *good life* here flow into an *eternall life*, without any consideration, what manner of *death* wee dye."

More frequently in Donne, however, we encounter the loose sentence, which is paratactic, episodic, serial, and seems in

"Deaths Duell" the aptest form to describe the unending triumph of death. And the sentence that does this best in the sermon is this one: "Wee have a *winding sheete* in our Mothers wombe, which growes with us from our conception, and we come into the world, wound up in that winding sheet, for wee come to *seeke a grave*; And as prisoners discharg'd of actions may lye for fees; so when the *wombe* hath discharg'd us, yet we are bound to it by *cordes* of flesh, by such a *string*, as that wee cannot goe thence, nor stay there." At this point, Donne has already invited us, his congregation, to imagine the infant in the womb, sightless and without sound, being "*fed with blood*" and "fitted for *workes of darkenes*." Why so monstrous, vampiric even? Because the child is like a worm that feeds on the body of its mother; but also resembles a corpse in the grave, that breeds then kills worms when the body is spent. A grotesque chain of associations is forged here, of which our sentence is the last rotten link, with its suggestion that the caul or amniotic membrane is itself a shroud, and the umbilical cord a chain by which at birth we are imprisoned. At the end of the sentence, it's clear not only that death rules in the midst of life—a predictable enough idea—but that life is exactly a state of being-between, almost undead.

Thrilled on its way by the already complete metaphor in the first clause, the logic of the sentence is inexorable, delirious. "Which," "and," "for": a hideous plausibility is being built here, soon to be mirrored in the "and," "so," "yet" of the second half of the sentence. It's possible to admire—that is, to fear and love—this sentence solely for the sleek, dire phrase at its centre: "for wee come to seeke a grave." It might almost have served on its own, given how forcibly Donne has already insisted that death is present from conception. Instead, either side of this phrase, there hang more unwieldy images, barely contained by the syntax of argument. The legal metaphor—the discharged prisoner still has costs to pay, so remains in prison—is straight out of Donne the poet and student of law. But the remainder is more curious, even awkward, with its odd shift from plural to singular ("cordes" to "string") and its weak, stringy phrasing: "as that wee cannot go thence." In spite of various symmetries—the strong metaphors, the prepositions and conjunctions—I do not think the two halves of the sentence are equal. The first, ending at the grave, sounds all of a piece, held together by the newborn wail of all those *w*'s. The second part seems fractured by that extra semicolon, even if we know that it's perfectly conventional for the time—the rhetorical punctuation (like Donne's frequent *italics*) pointing more to sound than grammatical sense.

In fact, in certain editions of "Deaths Duell," the sentence is cloven after "*seeke a grave*" and becomes two sentences; the first, I suppose, is "better" than the second, sufficient and entire unto itself. In another version published not long after Donne's death, our sentence is conjoined with the previous one, which already tells of "the death of the wombe" and "the manifold

31

deaths of this *worlde*." And in still another text—the rendering favoured by the editors of the Oxford University Press edition of all the sermons—fully four (or possibly five) shorter sentences are gathered into one long one: a paratactic heap of language that makes a funeral of birth, a mother's labour of life itself, and a swelling graveside mound of dirt out of such thoughts and their expression.

I remain attached to the version above, which happens to be the first I read. Its morbid extravagance, its botched symmetry, its alliteration, its repetitions—womb and winding sheet, the doubled discharge—all seem to dramatize thought itself. (It's these "peculiar convolutions," wrote Mario Praz, that keeps us coming back to Donne.) Perhaps the insight is swifter and more wittily expressed in the first half, but no matter. Or perhaps that is the point, because by the end of the sentence we are left hanging—or *depending*, as Donne liked to say. (Unable to advance or return, dangling or buried, doesn't he sound now like one of those fretful, stilled narrators out of the late works of Samuel Beckett?) At the end of the sermon, Donne asked his listeners to *depend* upon the image of Christ crucified, just as he *depended* from the Cross. "There wee leave you in that *blessed dependency*," he said, knowing very soon his own cord would be cut.

O Altitudo

"Time which antiquates Antiquities, and hath an art to make dust of all things, hath yet spared these *minor* Monuments."

—SIR THOMAS BROWNE

"FEW PEOPLE LOVE THE WRITINGS of Sir Thomas Browne, but those who do are of the salt of the earth." So wrote Virginia Woolf in the *TLS* in 1923. The admirers of Browne, the seventeenth-century physician and essayist, composer of a prose of astonishing stateliness, have included Thomas De Quincey, Herman Melville, Henry David Thoreau, Emily Dickinson, Jorge Luis Borges and William H. Gass. And of course Woolf, who in another essay, two years later, wrote: "We are in the presence of sublime imagination; now rambling through one of the finest lumber rooms in the world—a chamber stuffed from floor to ceiling with ivory, old iron, broken pots, urns, unicorns' horns, and magic glasses full of emerald lights and blue mystery." (This last image recalls "Blue and Green," Woolf's strange miniature fiction of a few years earlier, with its descriptions of two glass ornaments on a mantelpiece—

the first "faint blue with the veils of madonnas.") Reading Browne makes you want to write like this, piling up riches and curiosities, though it is easy to forget that his own writing is not very visual, and he is surprisingly prudent with his metaphors. The dramas in Browne's sentences, when they are not strictly to do with scientific or spiritual truth, are sonic, metrical, a matter of rhythm and cadence. Whether he is writing about natural history, peculiarities of religious belief, or archaeological discoveries, you can see in his prose the elements enchained and slowly moving. Like many of his modern readers, I first found Browne in W. G. Sebald's *The Rings of Saturn*. His sentences, Sebald writes, are like "processions or a funeral cortège in their sheer ceremonial lavishness."

I have chosen here one of Browne's best-known sentences. (*Chosen* is not exactly the word; the sentence has been with me—in notebooks at first, then known by heart—for over twenty years.) And why not? He is still very little read, despite recent biographies and new editions of works such as *Religio Medici* and *Hydriotaphia*, from which this sentence comes. Outside of scholarly discussions, it is hard to escape clichés about his "ornate" or "baroque" style, or about his teeming mind, a cabinet of ancient and contemporary curiosities. Hard to stick close to the sentences themselves, rather than pointing at them from an admiring distance, like those figures in sixteenth- or seventeenth-century engravings who gesture with hand or cane towards the obscure treasures in a *Wunder-*

kammer. Here is our priceless sentence again: "Time which antiquates Antiquities, and hath an art to make dust of all things, hath yet spared these *minor* Monuments." The phrase "antiquates Antiquities" is a metaphysical pun, not very far removed from the kind of thing you might find in Donne. The phrase seems to say more than that time turns things (including bodies) into artefacts—instead time accelerates what is already aged, actively intensifies decay. Antiquity *squared.* Coming before the comma, "antiquates Antiquities" is also an example of the kind of classical Latin cadence with which skilled writers of Browne's time had learned to terminate their clauses or sentences. The regular, but not too regular, appearance of such polysyllables gives to this sort of prose an elegant flow or *cursus.* "Antiquates Antiquities" is balanced at the end of the sentence by "spared these *minor* Monuments." And in between? The clause in the middle is a plain array of ten monosyllables—"and hath an art to make dust of all things"—of frankly biblical clarity. And over the whole sentence rhythm prevails, unstoppable like the advance of time.

Hydriotaphia, Urne-Buriall concerns a cache of Bronze Age burial urns unearthed in Norfolk. Browne takes these archaeological discoveries (which he thought were Roman) as occasion for an erudite, searching essay on funerary customs and so also on death. The thrust of his disquisition: the variety of practices—burying the dead or burning them, immuring above ground, with or without grave goods—is to be wondered at, and not judged from any one religious or historical vantage. But these customs are all carried out to no avail, at least on earth. No matter how elaborate the ritual or secure the interment, our fate is to be forgotten. The language in which Browne says this, however, is indelible, his lofty sentences lasting longer than his own grave. In 1840, in St Peter Mancroft Church in Norfolk, Browne's supposedly final resting place was disturbed, and the sexton George Potter took the opportunity to pilfer the skull and sell it. It was reburied in 1922. Meanwhile, Browne's sentences persisted. Sentences schooled on the language of the Bible: "Playstered and whited Sepulchres were anciently affected in cadaverous and corruptive Burials…" Or cast in a vocabulary that delicately negotiates between exactitude, euphemism and metaphor: "Christians have handsomely glossed the deformity of death, by careful consideration of the body, and civil rights which take off brutall terminations." Sentences that live on, deathless—for every sentence written is a sort of ghost—in the face of universal forgetting: "Oblivion is not to be hired: The greater part must be content to be as though they had not been, to be found in the Register of God, not in the record of man."

Daguerreotype, &c.

"Already, in this year 1845, what by the procession through fifty years of mighty revolutions among the kingdoms of the earth, what by the continual development of vast physical agencies,—steam in all its applications, light getting under harness as a slave for man, powers from heaven descending upon education and accelerations of the press, powers from hell (as it might seem, but these also celestial) coming round upon artillery and the forces of destruction,—the eye of the calmest observer is troubled; the brain is haunted as if by some jealousy of ghostly beings moving amongst us; and it becomes too evident that, unless this colossal pace of advance can be retarded (a thing not to be expected), or, which is happily more probable, forces in the direction of religion or profound philosophy, that shall radiate centrifugally against this storm of life so perilously centripetal towards the vortex of the merely human, left to itself, the natural tendency of so chaotic a tumult must be to evil; for some minds to lunacy, for others to a reägency of fleshly torpor."

—THOMAS DE QUINCEY

THOMAS DE QUINCEY is among the most endearing and infuriating writers of the nineteenth century. Endearing because De Quincey, whose *Confessions of an English Opium-Eater* is now his only well-known work, was an immoderately productive author who managed always to be on the verge of creative, physical and financial collapse. Infuriating for the same reasons: he could not settle his genius, materially or psychologically, for long enough to compose a single great sustained book. Spending his paradoxical energies on (to name only a handful of his chosen genres) autobiography, literary criticism, history, fiction, metaphysics and political economy, De Quincey also made a cottage industry out of his own vulnerability; his strongest writings, *Confessions* included, are about his weakness and susceptibility. All his adult life he was on the run from addiction, debt and the waves of grief and regret that periodically flooded his life. Unlike his fretting financial situation, the addiction and unhappiness were at least fuel for his magnificent prose. Paid by the page for most of his writings, De Quincey turned the exhausting metier of the periodical essayist into a phantasmagoric machine, capable of producing, at the suggestion of a deadline, fee and space to fill, the strangest prose effects of his time.

"Impassioned prose," Virginia Woolf called it, in an essay of that title. She meant that De Quincey's sentences—more than anything, he was a composer of sentences—not only described or expressed his fits of thought and feeling, but were themselves excited, infused, replete at the levels of their logic, rhythms, syntax, word choice and punctuation. Gorged and engorged. In his most high-flown passages, it was hard to tell De Quincey's prose from poetry. (Woolf was preparing her essay on De Quincey when she wrote to Vita Sackville-West: "my God Vita, if you happen to know do wire whats the essential difference between prose and poetry—It cracks my poor brain to consider.") Sir Thomas Browne is similarly impassioned, according to Woolf; also Ruskin, Emily Brontë, Thomas Carlyle and Walter Savage Landor. I would add Poe, Melville and Gass to the list: writers drunk on the almost erotic possibilities of their sentences. It is not really a matter of beauty or elegance, though a strangely lucid control of the sentence might be the first thing one admires in these writers. Something else, a grand engaging awkwardness, is soon felt; the sentence does not lose its way exactly, but somewhere forgets itself, and the reader slips with it, smiling. It might be a case of a metaphor too far, a turn of phrase that will not easily give up its sense, or a series of embedded clauses, like steps axed in glacier ice, from which the writer struggles confidently to descend again.

This sentence arrives early in De Quincey's "Introductory Notice" to the essay—or is it essays? prose-poem cycle? autobiographical fantasia?—that he titled *Suspiria De Profundis*. Later he admits that in this work, and others, he proceeds by digression or deviation, his reflective asides or narrative distractions threatening to choke his text like a parasitic plant growing on the trunk or limb of a tree. The parasitism is quite deliberate—the vagrant movement of De Quincey's prose and the attendant matter it discovers is all of the point, and gives to his work its picturesque attractions. To object to his way of writing, says De Quincey, is to behave like those impatient metropolitan visitors to the Lake District who are constantly asking the shortest route to the town of Keswick. After they have inquired of local innkeepers, and the postilions of regional stagecoaches, such characters are apt to put the same question to De Quincey, and receive a pointed reply: "the shortest of all possible tours would seem, with submission, never to have left London."

I'm attracted and confused by the phrase "what by," repeated in the opening lines: "Already...what by...what by...the eye is troubled." Wouldn't *by* have done the same job? What does *what* refer to? I'm not sure that we ever find out: the grammar of the sentence seems to simplify as it goes on, squandering the oblique expectations in *what by*, which has a Browne-like sense of expectation, as though a clause will arrive at the end to resolve all. Other elements that appeal: the twinned comma-dashes where now we would use plain dashes. (We might quibble over whether they should be short "en" or longer "em" dashes, and have spaces either side, or not: largely a controversy of British convention versus American.) In fact, so thoroughly unheard of is the once common comma-dash today, that in 2003 the editors of the most recent edition of De Quincey's *Works* replaced his with simple dashes (of the British sort). But I'm working from my late father's 1950s edition of

Confessions of an English Opium-Eater, which has *Suspiria* appended, and so there they are,—the comma-dashes like little hooks and lines either side of an aside,—snagging my attention. My father's copy is responsible also for the diaeresis (not an umlaut) in "reägency," the like of which you are unlikely to find outside of the exactingly, but eccentrically, punctuated pages of *The New Yorker*.

De Quincey was fifty-eight in 1844, when he started work on *Suspiria De Profundis*: a quarter of a century on from the brief, digressive masterpiece of the *Confessions*. In the earlier book, he says, the story of the author's opium addiction was an excuse to speak about a more profound matter: "The object of that work was to reveal something of the grandeur which belongs *potentially* to human dreams." The present work will continue these investigations; the dream, De Quincey writes, is "the one great tube through which man communicates with the shadowy." *Suspiria*, which he plans to publish in regular instalments in *Blackwood's* magazine, will be (so he hopes) the prose apotheosis of his late-Romantic adventure in the realm he is already calling (before anybody else) the *subconscious*. The essays will perform, for a Victorian audience living in the era of steam and speed and mechanical reproduction, a communion with the ageless mysteries of the inner self. The result, which circumstances and temperament conspired to ensure De Quincey never finished, is a work peculiarly haunted—by memories and losses, by a fear that impassioned prose, to which

41

he has devoted his life, is no longer possible, or desired, in the distractible modern world into which he is surprised to find he has survived. All of this is present in this long, involuted sentence from the opening paragraph of *Suspiria*.

The first essay, on "The Affliction of Childhood," deposits De Quincey in a sunlit room of his childhood, where his sister Elizabeth lies, recently dead at the age of nine. (Another sister, Jane, had died at three.) Thomas, who is six, has crept into the room to see Elizabeth's beloved face for the last time; soon doctors will arrive to perform an autopsy, laying waste to her skull, searching for the disease of the brain that has killed her. For now, another violent invasion is taking place, in De Quincey's own mind: "The terrific grief which I passed through drove a shaft for me into the worlds of death and darkness which never again closed, and through which it might be said that I ascended and descended at will, according to the temper of my spirits." He suffers vivid dreams and visions, in which as he gets older the pains of this and other losses will revive, curiously mixed with each other and with more occult, artistic or literary apparitions.

De Quincey will forget nothing, it will all be inscribed in his mind as if in a palimpsest: a manuscript whose letters, words and lines have been scraped away and overwritten, but remain faintly legible. De Quincey's memories are also weirdly influenced or strangely translated by his ability to conjure visions, as easily in lucid daylight as in his dreams at night.

"The faculty of shaping images in the distance, out of slight elements, and grouping them after the yearnings of the heart, aided by a slight defect in my eyes, grew upon me at this time." He is still a boy, the nightmares of opium addiction are many years away, but already De Quincey is seeing things. (Fleur Jaeggy, writing about De Quincey's childhood, puts it like this: "Dreams of 'terrific grandeur' had settled on the nursery. *A delectatio morosa* had clawed its way in.") Seated in church he looks up at the stained-glass windows, and the scenes there turn into visions of dying children in glowing white beds.

Among these visions, later in life, are versions of himself. In the *Suspiria* essay titled "The Apparition of the Brocken," De Quincey describes the "Brocken spectre": a meteorological phantom, most often seen at altitude, in which the greatly enlarged shadow of an observer is thrown upon mist or fog, and accompanied by a halo or "glory" of coloured light. In his poem "Constancy to an Ideal Object," Coleridge had described "an image with a glory round its head;/The enamoured rustic worships its fair hues,/Nor knows he makes the shadow, he pursues!" In James Hogg's 1824 novel *The Private Memoirs and Confessions of a Justified Sinner*, the spectre is one manifestation of the theme of the uncanny double, which later exercised Poe, Dostoevsky and R. L. Stevenson. Here is De Quincey's version: "The spectre takes the shape of a human figure, or, if the visitors are more than one, then the spectres multiply." Which is also what they do in *Suspiria De Profundis*,

43

where many phantom stand-ins for the writer's most profound self are to be found. In some places, De Quincey names this recurring figure the Dark Interpreter: it appears in his dreams, where it speaks, sometimes repeating what in waking life he has already thought or said, and sometimes surprising him with attitudes and feelings he did not know he harboured. Like the spectre of the Brocken, these ghosts are also confessors: "You are now satisfied that the apparition is but a reflex of yourself; and, in uttering your secret feelings to *him*, you make this phantom the dark symbolic mirror for reflection to the daylight what else must be hidden forever."

But first, before any of these subtle apparitions float onstage: the sentence, into whose folds are tucked so many of the visionary themes of *Suspiria*. The sentence demands patience; it is like waiting for a photograph to develop. What else are De Quincey's digressions—his deferrals and divagations—if not a chemical process into which a sentence, or a whole essay, is plunged and emerges transformed, assuming its final clarity? Photography is both one of the sentence's themes, and the guiding metaphor by which the thing is organized—the whole of *Suspiria* too. The argument of the first paragraph: that dreaming has declined among the modern, agitated English, the faculty of vision or imagination been vitiated. By what? By the supremacy of the steam engine in agriculture, industry and transport; by the proliferation of printed matter, in which De Quincey the prolific magazine writer is implicated; by advances, if that is the word, in the destructive power of artillery. And by "light getting under harness as a slave for man"—in other words, as De Quincey's delightfully terse (down to its ampersand) footnote tells us, the invention of Louis Daguerre's photographic process, which was announced in 1839. *Daguerreotype, &c.*

The sentence and its footnote contain the only explicit mentions of photography—of the definitive chemical fixing of images—that I know of in his published writings. And yet, photography is really everywhere in De Quincey's work, as a half-buried metaphor for the action of memory and imagination. The dream, he writes, is "the magnificent apparatus which forces the infinite into the chambers of a human brain, and throws dark reflections from eternities below all life upon the mirrors of that mysterious *camera obscura*—the sleeping mind." That mind is like a camera, albeit a camera that cannot yet make permanent the images that appear there. Except: for De Quincey they *are* permanent; he is convinced that "there is no such thing as forgetting possible to the human mind." It is as if the dreaming brain has secretly, all along, been hinting at this possibility of a permanent visual record or archive, but we have not known it. Most minds are incapable of De Quincey's proto-photographic recall: "Faces begin soon (in Shakespeare's fine expression) to 'dislimn'; features fluctuate; combinations of features unsettle. Even the expression becomes a mere idea that you can describe to another, but not an image that you can reproduce for yourself."

His mind is like a camera that captures and keeps everything, every image imprinted on the supersensitive palimpsest of the brain: it all comes back to him like a procession of spectres or phantoms. The mind is like a camera, and the camera is like—what? Now we arrive at the innermost mystery of the sentence itself; here it is, almost dead centre: "the brain is haunted as if by some jealousy of ghostly beings moving amongst us." The meaning of this statement—a clause that might have been a great sentence in itself—seems clear: technology, whether in transport, printing or photography, has suddenly, as we near the middle of the nineteenth century, surrounded us with apparitions: teeming urban travellers, the multiplied voices of the periodical press, the miraculous faces and figures in the new Daguerreotypes. As a reader, I understand the image: modernity breeds phantoms. As a writer, I want to know: what does De Quincey mean by "some jealousy of ghostly beings"? What "jealousy"?

Jealous has been, historically, a more capacious, more generous, word than it is today. Where it now applies almost solely to a proprietorial or envious feeling, the word used to express a wider variety of anxieties or kinds of apprehension. To be jealous, so the dictionary tells us, has meant to be "suspicious, apprehensive of evil, fearful." In Thomas Middleton's 1607 play *Five Gallants*: "My master is very jealous of the pestilence." It can mean doubtful or mistrustful, as in Shakespeare's *Julius Caesar*: "That you do love me, I am nothing jealous." Or it may denote a type of vigilance. In 1843, a year or so before De Quincey began writing *Suspiria De Profundis*, Poe had published his strange, psychologically suggestive story "The Purloined Letter." A piece of correspondence embarrassing to royalty has gone missing; a minister is suspected, and a search is carried out of his rooms. Before the purloined letter is found hidden in plain sight, the most intense surveillance is brought to bear on the apartment and environs. Or rather, says Poe, even to the gaps between cobblestones in the courtyard is directed "the most jealous scrutiny of the microscope."

I have been wondering for years what exactly this phrase, "some jealousy of ghostly beings," could mean, but have only now, as I'm writing, thought to solve the mystery by just looking the thing up. Perhaps I had wrestled enough with the serpentine grammar of the sentence; maybe I wanted to keep in mind, and in the mind of the sentence, an essential ambiguity. I think I liked the idea that "jealousy" might in fact be the collective noun, De Quincey's coinage or not, for a group of ghosts. Odd behaviour, to want the sentence to be *more* eccentric, or even to make less sense, than is already peculiarly the case. Because the "jealousy" is not the only enigmatic thing about the sentence. (There, we have solved it, it means anxiety: the ghostly beings have not yet appeared, we only fear their arrival.) The rest of the sentence is devoted to keeping the ghosts at bay. Mechanical modernity will not be slowed, let alone reversed, no matter how much De Quincey the natural

47

conservative (and avowed Tory) would wish it so. In the second half of the sentence, another sort of apparition takes over. Modernity is now a sort of celestial storm, something like the nebulae about which contemporary astronomy could not decide: were they flying apart with the chaotic energy of a cosmic explosion, or condensing, out of ignoble gas or vapour, into new heavenly bodies? In 1846, De Quincey published an essay, "System of the Heavens as Revealed by Lord Rosse's Telescopes," in which he considers the "nebular hypothesis": the idea, argued by William Herschel and others, that there existed a nebulous fluid out of which stars would eventually resolve. An engraving of the Great Nebula in Orion illustrates De Quincey's text, and he asks his readers to turn to it and see if they do not also see what he sees: a monstrous celestial head, resembling the figure of Death in *Paradise Lost.* "You see a head thrown back, and raising its face (or eyes, if eyes it had) in the very anguish of hatred to some unknown heavens. What *should* be its skull wears what *might* be an Assyrian tiara, only ending behind in a floating train. This head rests upon a beautifully developed neck and throat. All power being given to the awful enemy, he is beautiful where he pleases, in order to point and envenom his ghostly ugliness." Another ghost, another phantasm, another figure travelled out of troubled dreams to haunt his waking hours.

De Quincey was the only writer among the English Romantics to have his photograph taken. In 1850, he sat for the Edinburgh portrait photographer James Howie, whose rooftop studio was situated high above Prince's Street. (An engraving from a few years earlier shows Howie on the roof, in the open air, crouched at his camera while his sitter lounges in the sunshine. It's unclear if De Quincey, then aged sixty-five, climbed the four flights to this eyrie, or whether Howie descended to meet his celebrated subject.) In the picture, the crop-haired author looks away from us and purses his mouth, perhaps a little testily, or maybe just growing stiff during the long exposure. Later that year, an engraving from the daguerreotype appeared in the Edinburgh periodical *The Instructor*, and De Quincey wrote to the editor James Hogg (son of the writer):

I am much obliged to you for communicating to us (that is, to my daughters and myself) the engraved portrait, enlarged from the daguerreotype original. The engraver, at least, seems to have done his part ably. As to one of the earlier artists concerned, viz. the sun of July, I suppose it is not allowable to complain of *him*, else my daughters are inclined to upbraid him with having made the mouth too long.

The Exaltation of Lucy Snowe

"The drug wrought."

—Charlotte Brontë

THIS ECONOMICAL SENTENCE—THERE is something affronting or mischievous about its brevity—appears in chapter 38 of Charlotte Brontë's 1853 novel *Villette*. The book is less well known and less romantic (or Romantic) than *Jane Eyre*, but is in many respects the more ambitious novel. It is the story of one Lucy Snowe: a seemingly shy, melancholic young woman who is passed around among relatives and benefactors until she is engaged as a lowly schoolteacher in the Belgian town of Villette, which is transparently Brontë's stand-in for Brussels. Here Lucy despairs of her vain, lazy female pupils, is bullied by the school's proprietor Madame Beck, and falls in love—she will not admit it outright to the reader—with the schoolmaster, Paul Emanuel. Lucy is one of the least reliable narrators in nineteenth-century fiction: though she insists on her own timid and naive character, this little nervous subject inexorably asserts herself, and gets her way.

Lucy Snowe is also, to a large and detailed degree, Charlotte Brontë. Aged nineteen, Brontë had become a teacher at Roe Head girls' school, and felt the great loss of the freedom to imagine, and to write, that she and her siblings, in spite of the rigours and tragedies of their home, had enjoyed at Haworth. (While working and living at Roe Head, Brontë sent a letter, seeking encouragement as a writer, to the Poet Laureate, Robert Southey, and received a dismissive reply recommending she "take care of over-excitement, and endeavour to keep a quiet mind.") In February of 1842, Charlotte and Emily Brontë travelled to Brussels to study French at the Pensionnat Héger, near the Royal Park. The boarding school for girls was run by Claire Héger, and a school for boys, next door, by her husband Constantin. In the autumn, the sisters' aunt Elizabeth Branwell died, and they returned home, but in the new year M. Héger wrote to their father, hoping to welcome Charlotte back, this time as a teacher. Later, Brontë wrote: "I returned to Brussels after Aunt's death against my conscience—prompted by what then seemed to me an irresistible impulse—I was punished for my selfish folly by a total withdrawal of happiness and peace of mind." It seems she had fallen in love with Constantin Héger, though that is putting it too crudely: her suffering was as much composed of loneliness, and frustration at unfulfilled literary ambitions, as it was emotional attachment or guilty, adulterous desire.

Brontë described her malady more precisely: she suffered, she said, from "*hypochondria.*" The word did not mean, or did not mean only, what it does today—it included a physical (chiefly digestive) component, but was in essence close to what we would call depression, with a strong admixture of anxiety. In the Brontës' family library at Haworth, there was a medical manual, Thomas John Graham's *Modern Domestic Medicine*, published in 1826. The hypochondriac, Graham writes, "is tormented with a visionary or exaggerated sense of pain, or some concealed disease; a whimsical dislike of particular persons, places or things; groundless apprehensions of personal danger or poverty; a general listlessness and disgust; or an irksomeness and weariness of life." In *Jane Eyre*, Rochester diagnoses as hypochondria Jane's fears and fancies on the night before they are supposed to be married. William Crimsworth, the orphaned, schoolteacher protagonist of *The Professor*, also suffers a brief attack of pre-nuptial hypochondria: "A horror of great darkness fell upon me." In Lucy Snowe, like her creator, the illness appears more ingrained; it is worsened by solitude and unfulfilled desires, writerly as well as romantic, and it sometimes finds obscure expression in the darkest imaginings.

The most dramatic of Lucy's hypochondriac fits happens late in the novel—the chapter is titled "Cloud"—when Paul

Emanuel has announced he is leaving the school, and Lucy fears he will vanish without another word passing between them. The whole establishment, staff and pupils, knows the source of Lucy's distress, but Madame Beck insists on the pretence that she has a headache, and so hurries her to bed with a draught of laudanum: opium mixed with alcohol. But Beck has miscalculated—"I know not whether Madame had over-charged or under-charged the dose"—and instead of sending Lucy to sleep the drug enlivens her, mind and body. "I became alive to new thought—to reverie peculiar in colouring. A gathering call ran among the faculties, their bugles sang, their trumpets rang an untimely summons. Imagination was roused from her rest, and she came forth impetuous and venturous. With scorn she looked on Matter, her mate—'Rise!' she said."

Lucy gets up, dresses, and races out into the moonlit city, which is filled with extraordinary scenes. Edifices drawn from ancient Egyptian architecture have risen in the park: they are made of wood and plaster. A fête is under way, and citizens are abroad in their finery, enjoying gaily illumined entertainments, or observing the crowd from carriages. Nobody seems to notice Lucy Snowe, not even her godmother, or Madame Beck, or the priest to whom Lucy has lately delivered an anxious confession. Hours pass like this, and the reader may be quite unsure whether any of it is meant to be real. Brontë told her first biographer, the novelist Elizabeth Gaskell, that she had never taken opium, and so had to invent the atmosphere as well as specifics of Lucy Snowe's ordeal. She did not tell Gaskell that she had read Thomas De Quincey's *Confessions of an English Opium-Eater*, from which it is easy to conclude she might have borrowed the visionary texture of the whole, as well as such startling orientalist detail as the pyramids and sphinxes that seem to come straight from certain engravings by Piranesi that fascinated De Quincey.

"The drug wrought." In the "Cloud" chapter, or elsewhere in *Villette*, Brontë's prose is not exactly the digressive equal of De Quincey's elaborate style. Still, this is an astonishingly simple sentence with which to introduce the extravagant visions of Lucy Snowe. Or is it? Short guttural sentence in which it is hard, saying it aloud or hearing it in your head, not to elongate "wrought," awkwardly or self-consciously, as if to make up for the fact there seems to be something missing. The drug wrought *what*? Nowadays we usually come across "wrought" as a past participle: a gate of *wrought* iron; an artefact, idea, image, plan, or a sentence perhaps, that has been well (or cunningly) *wrought*. Hardly ever do we stop to ask what the original verb is, from which "wrought" derives. Is it "wreak"? As in: "to wreak havoc" and "they wrought havoc." In fact, as the OED tells us, there is some confusion at work here, and "work" is exactly the word that matters. "To work havoc" is a variant, now rare, and gives us the clue: "wrought," among other things, is the plain past tense of the verb *to work*, and in more than one sense of making or fashioning. "Wrought" may apply (or has applied, historically) to movement, labour, function, shaping or manipulation.

And so Brontë's modest sentence might mean: the drug worked, or went to work, performed its usual or intended function. The sentence could as easily mean that the drug *went to work on*, influenced or manipulated, the raw material of Lucy Snowe's imagination—it *worked her* as though she were metal to be moulded or beaten, stone or wood to be carved. Brontë might have said instead: "The drug wrought me, or wrought my mind." Which in turn suggests the sense of making or inventing: "The drug wrought scenes or visions." The glorious and sinister diorama of Lucy Snowe's night in the Royal Park: it has all been *wrought* by opium. Or is it rather, again: the reality *worked* by opium, heightened or intensified? All of these meanings are present, all of them complementing and contending with each other, inside this tiny, concentrated sentence. To Mrs. Gaskell, Brontë said that before writing the "Cloud" chapter she lay half awake each night, trying to imagine what an overdose of laudanum would feel like, until she woke one morning with the conviction she had got it right. Undrugged, she wrought. Like De Quincey, who had really been there, Brontë describes the realm of the sedative, pain-killing drug as if it's instead both stimulant and hallucinogen. As if, that is, its power is creative, artistic, literary. As if the sentence contains a pun: the *drug wrote*.

A History of the Lights and Shadows

"Our moods are apt to bring with them images which succeed each other like the magic-lantern pictures of a doze; and in certain states of dull forlornness Dorothea all her life continued to see the vastness of St. Peter's, the huge bronze canopy, the excited intention in the attitudes and garments of the prophets and evangelists in the mosaics above, and the red drapery which was being hung for Christmas spreading itself everywhere like a disease of the retina."

—GEORGE ELIOT

THIS SENTENCE—HOW else to say it?—embarrasses me, and not only because I could never hope to match its wisdom and its rhythms and that weird image at the end. In the spring of 1991, I was in the final year of a degree in English literature at University College Dublin. In a fit of enthusiasm at the start of the first term, I had gotten myself elected as student representative at departmental meetings. I was twenty-one years old, and all ardent for the months ahead, which I hoped would lead on to graduate school. For the first time in my life I was primed for some hard work, eager for academic success. I took a class on "Narrative and Interpretation" in the nineteenth century, and flung myself at novels and stories by the Brontës, James Hogg, Edgar Allan Poe, and Henry James. I had not yet opened *Middlemarch* (1872) when a group of fellow students came up to me after a lecture and broached the subject of Eliot's novel.

Unlike the rest of the course, *Middlemarch* was being taught by a visiting professor from Texas, and word had gone around that this character was attached to the Great Books Program back in Austin. Knowing nothing about the pedagogical history of these programmes in the United States, my friends and I delighted in mocking a naïve allegiance to the sturdy canon. We imagined this dude and his pals all sitting around in Stetsons, occasionally slamming a meaty palm on some classic volume and declaring: "It's a great book!" And so I didn't baulk when my classmates asked that I go see our professor and enquire, because they had grown afraid of its heft: Do we have to read all of *Middlemarch*? Might we not sample instead a few chapters that touched on our theme? I don't recall much about this shameful interview in his office, except the gales of laughter and an assurance that *Middlemarch* was nothing but narrative and interpretation.

Of course, it is something else too: a novel about sympathy in more than one sense. As a portrait—better, a panorama—of provincial life in England around 1830, *Middlemarch* is intimately concerned with how much its characters know about one another, the extent to which they can credit each other's interior lives, the capacities they own for understanding and indulgence. I'd been prepared for all of this—stock moral stuff in Victorian realism—but not for the way Eliot speaks of sympathy, or its absence: in strange and complex metaphors such as open and close our sentence. I was not expecting language like this, in which sympathy is physical or chemical as well as spiritual, moral, and aesthetic. Here is a sentence whose art as well as import demanded I become a more sympathetic reader—and person.

The twentieth chapter of *Middlemarch*, in which the sentence appears, finds Eliot's enthusiastic but limited young heroine Dorothea Brooke weeping alone in Rome. She has married the clergyman and scholar Edward Casaubon and discovered too late that her much older husband's intellectual inwardness, so attractive at first, disallows the learned and literary union she had anticipated. (Casaubon is also likely impotent, and incapable of completing his life's work, a "Key to All Mythologies.") They have come to Italy on honeymoon, and in her state of matrimonial defeat, Dorothea finds the sights pass in front of her eyes like a funeral procession. The spectacles of classical civilization and Catholic culture are enervating when they are not irritating: "her mind was continually sliding into inward fits of anger or repulsion, or else into forlorn weariness." And so Dorothea wanders alone through palaces and basilicas, amid colossal statues and crumbling ruins—all glowing with "the monotonous light of an alien world."

It might have been the light that struck me first in the sentence. The magic-lantern slides in the long opening clause: they recall dream images that loomed in the drugged brain of Thomas De Quincey half a century before. The unconscious mind, says the author of *Confessions of an English Opium-Eater*, is like the splendid mechanism of a phantasmagoria, projecting its horrors into the black-box theatre of the eye. And shouldn't we think also of Proust? Little Marcel sent to bed in the afternoon with a magic lantern to entertain him, watching on his bedroom wall the medieval romance of Genevieve of Brabant, whose betrayer Golo wears a red cloak. And what about Virginia Woolf, who wrote in "Modern Fiction" (1925): "Life is not a series of gig lamps symmetrically arranged; life is a luminous halo, a semi-transparent envelope surrounding us from the beginning of consciousness to the end." How odd (I should not have thought) to find George Eliot in this lineage of illuminating metaphors for mental life under modernity and modernism.

But wait, it's all much more complicated. Because even before we get to the semicolon—more on that creaky little hinge in a while—Eliot, or her nameless and all-seeing narrator, is already mixing her metaphors. The frieze of images in a distraught and distracted mind like Dorothea's: what is it like, exactly? A magic-lantern show, for sure, but not only or not

59

quite. The pictures are products of "a doze," which is to say that a mood is like a dream—they both make pictures, like a magic lantern. As J. Hillis Miller, one of her most astute scholarly readers, points out, this is typical of Eliot: her descriptions of one thing in terms of another will often suggest some further metaphorical turn or metonymic swerve. The milieu of *Middlemarch* is like a flowing body of water. Or it is like a web. Or perhaps a minutely scratched steel mirror or pier glass, to which narrator and reader alike must bring the weak light of understanding and sympathy—the scratches will seem to encircle our limited perspective on individuals and events. Maybe the world of the novel—and maybe the world—is like a densely woven fabric, and the best we can do is pick at its pattern in one place, hoping thereby to comprehend the whole.

Dorothea knows little of this; she simply stares and sobs. It is one of the arguments—if that is the word—of the novel: we all live according to guiding (and misguiding) metaphors, but we do not fully know it, let alone understand where they may take us. And the novelist herself? Eliot had borrowed the architectural and anatomical imagery for Dorothea's oppressed mind from her own travels in Italy in 1860. Here she is in her journal of that year, describing St Peter's: "The exterior of the cathedral itself is even ugly; it causes a constant irritation by its partial concealment of the dome. The first impression from the interior was perhaps at a higher pitch than any subsequent impression either of its beauty or vastness; but then, on later visits, the lovely marble, which has a tone at once subdued and warm, was half-covered with hideous red drapery."

In reality, the drapery was for Holy Week and not for Christmas, but there it is: the source of the real shock in Eliot's sentence. "Like a disease of the retina." You could say of this medical metaphor, which may have grown over years in the writer's mind or presented itself to her in a flash on considering her journal of 1860, that it is quite of a piece with other aspects of the novel. Until his researches are derailed by his own unhappy marriage, Eliot's idealistic young physician Tertius Lydgate devotes himself to a quest for the fundamental matter of which human organs are made. Optical metaphors are everywhere in *Middlemarch*, but dominate especially Lydgate's thoughts. Like the novel's narrator, he believes that authentic knowledge demands a constant movement between the panoramic and the microscopic view, between concentration and expansion: "There must be a systole and diastole in all inquiry." Readers of the novel get used to—perhaps many do not even notice—the way such metaphors migrate between the minds of the narrator and her characters.

How have we arrived at this image? Via, in that first clause, the generalizing and sententious tone that Eliot's narrator so often adopts. "Our moods are apt to bring with them," she tells us, and we must be brought with her, into the hall of mirrors that her metaphors make. There's a turn at the end of the first corridor, marked by the semicolon and the somewhat presumptuous, eliding "and," which demands that we keep on following, unquestioning, because we are now face to face with a concrete instance of the sentence's opening generalization. Except, except: all is now dreamlike and phantasmagorical. "Dull" and "forlorn" are favourite words of Eliot's—the latter is a reminder of Keats's "Ode to a Nightingale": "the very word is like a bell"—and they're attached precisely to the state Lydgate describes of moving between broad and narrow views. A kind of stupefaction or stupidity brings with it an alarming and even monstrous clarity, vividity. Real and mental objects loom, and look like other objects.

(Here is Elizabeth Bowen, eighty-eight years later in *A Time in Rome*, standing in front of the Fascist-classical Palazzo della Civiltà Italiana, with its six floors of grandiose arches, that Mussolini had built in Rome for his doomed 1942 World's Fair: "Later, while I was gazing at it from the central square, a safe distance, I saw a long file of German seminarists, in their scarlet *soutanes*, sweep up the terrace steps and into the arches—the effect was, a trickle of blood reversed, returning to the wound." And here is Bowen, in a more comic register, in *The Last September*, from 1929: "The dining-room was dark red, with a smoky ceiling, and Gerald said afterwards he had felt like a disease in a liver.")

Aged twenty-one, I thought I'd found the whole of George Eliot in a single sentence: a conviction almost as wrongheaded as Casaubon's belief in a key to mythologies or Lydgate's in his organic universal. But my mistake was also a lesson. I learned not to judge any writer by the broad categories—"Victorian," "realist"—too easily applied to their books. And I learned not to judge other readers, such as our professor with his beloved Great Books, and other humans in general, for their apparently conventional attitudes, when in fact they had done the hard work, the adventurous work, that I had not. But it was years later, when I had to teach *Middlemarch* myself, that I fully grasped the eccentricity of Eliot's "like a disease of the retina." Because the question is: whose retina? Eliot's? The narrator's? Dorothea's? The reader's? It's unclear where and when the spreading in question takes place: in St Peter's or in the memories of Dorothea and her inventor? Still, the image creeps into the mind, and its blindness and insight belong to all of us who convene in this capacious and mad sentence.

Traditions of Air

"It waked me at six, or a little before—then rolling incessantly, like railway luggage trains, quite ghastly in its mockery of them—the air one loathsome mass of sultry and foul fog, like smoke; scarcely raining at all, but increasing to heavier rollings, with flashes quivering vaguely through all the air, and at last terrific double streams of reddish-violet fire, not forked or zigzag, but rippled rivulets—two at the same instant some twenty to thirty degrees apart, and lasting on the eye at least half a second, with grand artillery-peals following; not rattling crashes, or irregular cracklings, but delivered volleys."

—JOHN RUSKIN

JOHN RUSKIN WAS FOUR DAYS AWAY from his sixty-sixth birthday when he delivered the lecture in which this sentence appears. His powers as a writer were not yet depleted; the autobiographical *Praeterita*, which is his last great work, remained to be written. But Ruskin's psychic weather was on the turn. In 1878 he suffered the first of several breakdowns, and his biographers have ventured the usual amateur diagnoses—was it paranoid schizophrenia, or manic-depressive illness? Late in 1878 he was unwell enough to miss the hearing, and verdict, in the infamous libel case the painter James McNeill Whistler had brought against him. (Ruskin accused Whistler in print of "flinging a pot of paint in the public's face"; the artist won damages of one farthing.) Ruskin recovered sufficiently to write and lecture again; in March of 1880 he spoke at the London Institution on the subject of snakes in art and life, in what is really a lecture all about form and the formless. Early in 1881, a second mental crisis overtook him. Further public controversy followed when Ruskin, who was more and more convinced of certain decadent and even fatal tendencies in Western civilization, engaged in polemics against contemporary science, industry and medicine.

Was Ruskin mad in February 1884, when on the 4th and 11th of the month (once again at the London Institution) he delivered the two talks that together make up "The Storm-Cloud of the Nineteenth Century"? Journalists from the *Times* and the *Pall Mall Gazette*, which reported the lectures, either implied as much or came right out with it, so that when Ruskin published the texts of his talks—first as pamphlets, then as a short book—he was forced to declare they had been "drawn up under the pressure of more imperative and quite otherwise directed work." In fact, he admitted, they were "thrown into form" (maybe form was the issue?) both "hastily" and "incautiously." It would have been quite like him, he said, to have written and spoken from his imagination or fancy. But not in this case. At any rate, he was quite able to tell healthy, accurate impressions from morbid invention or delusion. Ruskin, in other words, insisted he knew perfectly well if, or when, he had lost his mind. (Useful skill for any writer—imagine!) In "The Storm-Cloud of the Nineteenth Century" he had brought rationally to bear upon the world "a chemist's analysis, and a geometer's precision." To what end? Only "to bring to your notice a series of cloud phenomena, which, so far as I can weigh existing evidence, are peculiar to our own times."

Ruskin had been a close observer of clouds all his life. They were among the glories of nature, thus among the great challenges for painters and poets—also for writers of poetic prose. Formed and unformed, distinct and dissolving, the cloud was pure etheric becoming, but arrested in the sky, or at least appearing so. Clouds apprehended, clouds drawn, painted or described in writing: even before the arrival of photography, these were the film stills of the Romantic era. The cinema of weather, rolling past, gives us these fleetingly frozen shapes. No matter how blown about, however frayed at the edges by wind, or obscured to view by its own rain, a cloud, Ruskin insists, is always emphatically itself: "a cloud is where you see it, and isn't where you don't." At least, that is how things used to be:

In those old days, when weather was fine, it was luxuriously fine; when it was bad—it was often abominably bad, but it had its fit of temper and was done with it—it didn't sulk for three months without letting you see the sun,—nor send you one cyclone inside out, every Saturday afternoon, and another outside in, every Monday morning.

While we are poised here with Ruskin, sighing over the good old clouds of yestersky, consider the language by which he frames the virtuous and noble (important word, in Ruskin) bodies of the air. Observe the lucid, though also lacy, virtues of a sentence such as this:

> On any pure white, and practically opaque, cloud, or thing like a cloud, as an Alp, or Milan Cathedral, you can have cast by rising or setting sunlight, any tints of amber, orange, or moderately deep rose—you can't have lemon yellows, or any kind of green except in negative hue by opposition; and though by storm-light you may sometimes get the reds cast very deep, beyond a certain limit you cannot go,—the Alps are never vermilion colour, nor flamingo colour, nor canary colour; nor did you ever see a full scarlet cumulus of thunder-cloud.

The symmetries are awing in this sentence. Everything is balanced around the semicolon after "opposition," resting calmly on the twinned but not parenthetical dashes. In the opening clauses, Ruskin confects for us a cloud, adds some things that are like clouds (but are they? an Alp? Milan Cathedral?), then the happy accidents of colour, before he starts subtracting qualities in the second half of the sentence. (It happens, in fact, just before the semicolon.) Clouds are rarely symmetrical, of course, no more so than mountains or even cathedrals—but the almost perfect weighting of syntax and punctuation stands in, structure figuring substance, for the purity and discretion of the cloud. Which may prompt us to ask: just how noble and selfsame is this thing if it's subject to, or if it can only be truly grasped in, such allegorical extravagance?

So much for old-fashioned clouds. Something else has lately hovered into view, and shadows Ruskin's imagination like the sudden arrival of an alien spacecraft, stationary and sinister in the sky above the city where he speaks. He first saw it in 1871, on a walk out of Oxford. Since then, it has followed him from Sicily to the north of England: a dark and dirty cloud—"storm-cloud, or more accurately plague-cloud"—accompanied by an unsettling wind. The cloud is "a dry black veil," the wind "a wind of darkness." When they arrive, the sky is blackened instantly, and the wind starts up from any direction, even from all points at once, "attaching its own bitterness and malice to the worst characters of the proper winds of each quarter." This wind blows "*tremulously*": time and again in his diaries Ruskin has remarked the leaves outside his window, or in the woods when he has dared to go for a walk, shaking as if in anger, fear, distress. Here he is in a diary entry for the 22nd of June, 1876:

Thunderstorm; pitch dark, with no *blackness*,—but deep, high, *filthiness* of lurid, yet not sublimely lurid, smoke-cloud; dense manufacturing mist; fearful squalls of shivering wind, making Mr. Severn's sail quiver like a man in a fever fit—all about four, afternoon—but only two or three claps of thunder, and feeble, though near, flashes. I never saw such a dirty, weak, foul storm.

Recall his claim to scientific precision—Ruskin has had "solitude and leisure" enough, these past fifty years, to record his impressions of the heavens, and to know when the "traditions of air" have been traduced. The evidence is all above him but also on the ground: when the plague-wind blows, Ruskin finds his garden full of weeds gone to seed, and his roses "putrefied into brown sponges, feeling like dead snails." The proof, he tells his audience at the London Institution, is in his diaries, where a year before the lectures we find this: "yesterday a fearfully dark mist all afternoon, with steady, south plague-wind of the bitterest, nastiest, poisonous blight, and fretful flutter. I could scarcely stay in the wood for the horror of it." Adjectives pile up in the evidentiary archive of Ruskin's journals—also very striking metaphors: he looks aghast from his window at Brantwood, as the plague-wind blows "sheaves of lancets and chisels across the lake."

What is metaphoric and what is real, what fact and what figure, in "The Storm-Cloud of the Nineteenth Century"?

The distinction is as perilous for readers as it was for Ruskin, who could no longer sustain (if he had ever really managed it) a hard border between observation and imagination, or between—and here at last is where we start approaching our sentence—the kinds of language, the species of prose, that are fitting to each. What are we to make, for example, of his assertion that the cloud, while it "looks partly as if it were made of poisonous smoke," seems "more to me as if it were made of dead men's souls—such of them as are not yet gone where they have to go, and may be flitting hither and thither, doubting, themselves, of the fittest place for them"? Is that Christian surmise or spectral metaphor? Ruskin will not help us decide, except to say, in a reference to the dead of the Franco-Prussian War, that if the cloud *is* composed of dead souls, "there must be many above us, just now, displeased enough!" At such moments, one begins to think that Ruskin's prose—and maybe this lecture itself—is a rhetorical cloud, exquisitely formed and likely any moment to turn ragged, dark, unruly.

How easy it is to think of the prose of Victorian writers—especially the venerated, or formerly venerated, male essayists, those bearded oracles, orotund declaimers—as sculptors of extremely formal sentences, each one a more or less elaborate monument in the municipal cemetery that is an oeuvre as vast and (now mostly) unread as Ruskin's thirty-nine-volume *Works*. Easy, and easily but not always wrong. Annie Dillard makes this point eloquently in her book *Living by Fiction*. She is talking about "fine writing," which is a precious name to give to the work of writers as diverse as Browne, De Quincey, Proust, James, Woolf, Beckett—and Ruskin. Dillard intends a formal prose, for sure, but the more she describes it the stranger and less strictured it sounds.

> This is an elaborated, painterly prose. It raids the world for materials to build sentences. It fabricates a semi-opaque weft of language. It is a spendthrift prose, and a prose of means. It is dense in objects which pester the senses. It hauls in visual imagery of every sort; it strews metaphors about, and bald similes, and allusions to every realm. It does not shy from adjectives, nor even from adverbs. It traffics in parallel structures and repetitions; it indulges in assonance and alliteration.

We like to think of, and sometimes dismiss, such prose as decorous, controlled, when in fact "the old men in frock coats" were violently eager for power—their style is an energy, tirelessly, and sometimes carelessly, amassing the lumber of meaning.

As an instance, Dillard gives us this, from Ruskin's preface to *Modern Painters*: "Every alteration of the features of nature has its origin either in powerless indolence or blind audacity, in the folly which forgets, or in the insolence which desecrates, works which it is the pride of angels to know, and their privilege to love." Dillard's point is: yes, there is control here, which in prose often means the mastery of certain kinds of repetition. Repetitions promote a sense of seamlessness, and flow, and uniformity. There is Ruskin's alliteration ("powerless... pride... privilege") and (oh!) his more obvious assonance: "origin in powerless indolence... folly which forgets." There are the piled-up parallels, which sometimes demand an introductory "or," and sometimes just a comma. It is all of a piece—except, this kind of control also allows for the almost endless replication of its elements: more and more echoes in sound and sense, until the thing, the sentence, gets out of hand, cacophonous.

In Ruskin's earlier sentences you can see, or hear, his prose machinery (he would hate the metaphor) going complexly to work. Like many writers, as he got older his sentences became looser, less fretful to impress by their elaborate self-command. Virginia Woolf once wrote about him: "We find ourselves marvelling at the words, as if all the fountains of the English language had been set playing in the sunlight for our pleasure." The image seems appropriate to the sunlit descriptions in *The Stones of Venice*, and for the defences of Turner's misty canvasses in *Modern Painters*. What would the correct mechanical, or hydraulic, metaphor be for what has happened to Ruskin's sentences by the time of "The Storm-Cloud of the Nineteenth Century," and which perhaps had already occurred many times in his diaries? All I can think is that the fountains have been set to send out a more violent spray, or someone has introduced a foaming agent into the pools below. (Anne Carson: "Foam is the sign of an artist who has sunk his hands into his own story, and also of a critic storming and raging in his own deep theory.")

Let's look at and listen to the sentence again, but this time stand back so that it is framed by its diminutive neighbours. It is the 13th of August, 1879, and Ruskin is at Brantwood.

The most terrific and horrible thunderstorm, this morning, I ever remember. It waked me at six, or a little before—then rolling incessantly, like railway luggage trains, quite ghastly in its mockery of them—the air one loathsome mass of sultry and foul fog, like smoke; scarcely raining at all, but increasing to heavier rollings, with flashes quivering vaguely through all the air, and at last terrific double streams of reddish-violet fire, not forked or zigzag, but rippled rivulets—two at the same instant some twenty to thirty degrees apart, and lasting on the eye at least half a second, with grand artillery-peals following; not rattling crashes, or irregular cracklings, but delivered volleys. It lasted an hour, then passed off, clearing a little, without rain to speak of,—not a glimpse of blue,—and now, half-past seven, seems settling down again into Manchester devil's darkness.

You could get distracted by the categorical judgements in that first sentence, or be hooked (as in De Quincey) by the curious combination of dash and comma in the third sentence. But

73

frame the central patch of sentence-sky: what is going on in there? Or rather, first, what is not? The balance, the symmetry, the parallelisms: these have broken down, and in their place is a structure—built on what? On the vaguely chronological piling up of impressions, set off by dashes and semicolons and seemingly fast distinctions—not this, but that—which hardly conjure a vivid picture of the less than vivid scene. "It waked me at six, or a little before": the punctual start is already uncertain, and followed ("then rolling") by a parenthetical turn of ambiguous temporal import: does "then" mean *at that time* or *subsequently*? The comparison of thunder to the sound of rolling train carriages is perfectly conventional, though a little more insistent in the case of Ruskin, who took harder than most aesthetes of his age against the railways. (And why "luggage trains"?) There is something both weak and excessive about "quite ghastly in its mockery of them," which assumes either that the sound of a train is naturally repulsive to sense and sensibility, or that too keen a mimicry of same would sound ghastly. The problem may reside in the word "ghastly" itself, which summons something pallid, deathly, thus offensive to eye and not ear.

But there are other eccentricities, never mind of metaphor and simile. Back we come after the second dash—to what? The aside has served, as a comma would, to produce a dependent clause: "the air one loathsome mass of sultry and foul fog, like smoke." Fog, smoke or cloud: whatever this pall is made of it has blotted out any hope we may have of spotting a strong verb any time soon. Instead, after "smoke" and the semicolon, there is the raining and rolling and "flashes quivering vaguely through all the air." Strange phrase, that: "flashes quivering vaguely." Is it not in the nature of a flash that it should *flash* rather than *quiver*? But we're speaking here of lightning flashes, and isn't "quiver" an apt enough word for the zigzagging, dog-legging path of the flash as it forks to earth? Let's allow Ruskin his "quivering." But "quivering vaguely"? Are there not in fact yet fully formed forks of lightning? The next clause confirms it: streams of fire at last, but not forked, not zigzag—"rippled rivulets." We're back in the same obscure visual perplex as before; what kind of lightning forms in ripples or rivulets? At least, it seems, the accompanying thunder sounds out clearly, not "rattling" or "irregular"—but the adjectives suggest that this is mostly what Ruskin has been listening to: indeterminate sounds that mimic the nebulous forms of storm-cloud and plague-wind.

"While I have written this sentence the cloud has again dissolved itself"—maybe Ruskin was aware of a ragged affinity between the storm-cloud and his increasingly irregular sentences. Not to mention his own mind: in "The Storm-Cloud of the Nineteenth Century," one has the sense of an author unravelling with his prose. Ruskin's sentences shake themselves apart. His writing, in fact, had always been filled with images of intermittence, trembling or wavering. And he had always been ambivalent about such vibrations. In 1860, in *The Ethics of the Dust* (subtitled "Ten Lectures to Little Housewives on the Elements of Crystallization"), he has asked his audience of schoolgirls, and later his readers, to imagine "the mud or slime of a damp over-trodden path in the outskirts of a manufacturing town." With unthinkable slowness, like the floor of the sea or the sediments of lake and river, such filth will refine itself from mud into coal and then into precious stones. This image returns in "The Storm-Cloud of the Nineteenth Century" when Ruskin tells us "The leaf hears no murmur in the wind to which it wavers on the branches, nor can the clay discern the vibration by which it is thrilled into a ruby." This last phrase, "thrilled into a ruby," is exquisite—but quite the opposite process is at work in Ruskin's lectures on the storm-cloud, and already in the diaries on which he draws. Syntactically, rhythmically, tonally, the fractures and flaws—"inclusions," say the gemologists—are showing, the polished facets of Ruskin's prose are shivering, sliding, coming apart, turning particulate as he pores over his old diaries.

"My mind was book-bound and mist-mixed," writes William H. Gass in an essay on Emerson: it sounds like a description of Ruskin looking up anxiously from his diaries, towards the darkening sky. His sentences tremble, threaten to evanesce. Does this one know, any more than its author, who will before long lapse into silence and insanity, that it is quite so vulnerable? Perhaps it knows no more than the leaf, or the clay, or the wave that Ruskin had described, in *Modern Painters*, in a passage on the pathetic fallacy—the mistaken or excessive poetic imputation of life or agency into inanimate objects. "The foam is not cruel, neither does it crawl. The state of mind which attributes to it these characters of a living creature is one in which the reason is unhinged by grief." Can a sentence grieve as well as tell us about grief? It is how I think of the sentences in "The Storm-Cloud of the Nineteenth Century," tremulous things that look back at a world of purity and clarity, and find it wreathed in smoke.

Suppose a Sentence

"Supposing a certain time selected is assured, suppose it is even necessary, suppose no other extract is permitted and no more handling
is needed, suppose the rest of the message is mixed with a very long
slender needle and even if it could be any black border, supposing all
this altogether made a dress and suppose it was actual, suppose the
mean way to state it was occasional, if you suppose this in August
and even more melodiously, if you suppose this even in the necessary
incident of there certainly being no middle in summer and winter, suppose this and an elegant settlement a very elegant settlement is more
than of consequence, it is not final and sufficient and substituted."

—Gertrude Stein

She must have derived her fondness for the verb "to
suppose" from her study of logic and composition. At Harvard,
her teachers complained of her cavalier attitude to grammar,
but Gertrude Stein had always taken pleasure, she said later,
in learning and testing the rules: "I really do not know that
anything has ever been more exciting than diagramming sentences." Has any writer of English prose been so vocally affected

by the rigours and romance of the sentence? *How to Write*, which among other things may be a parody of a composition manual she was made to read as a student, is the book in which Stein's thoughts about the sentence are most complexly and completely expressed. "A sentence has wishes as they decide." "A sentence should be arbitrary it should not please be better." "A sentence is saved not any sentence no not any sentence at all not yet." And the mock-pedagogical imperative: "Now feebly commence a sentence."

"*Suppose a sentence*," Stein commands in her 1934 portrait of the artist and designer Christian Bérard:

Suppose a sentence.

How are ours in glass.

Glass makes ground glass.

A sentence of their noun.

How are you in invented complimented.

How are you in in favourite.

Thinking of sentences in complimented.

Sentences in in complimented in thank in think in sentences in think in complimented.

Sentences should not shrink. Complimented.

A sentence two sentences should not think complimented.

Complimented.

How do you do if you are to to well complimented.

A sentence leans to along.

Ambiguous word, "suppose," demanding in its various applications that we assume, presume, presuppose. But also imagine, posit, believe. And then again: imply, represent, require to exist. "Suppose a sentence" means, as in some instructive context—"Suppose a triangle..." "Suppose a man, X..."—*let us agree to the existence of this thing, at least for the moment, although we know it is an intellectual fiction, a purely experimental entity.* On the other hand, here the thing actually is, on the page: a supposition made concrete, plain and apprehensible. "Suppose" is in this case close to "invent": they both mean to forge, to fabricate mentally, to frame by imagination, and to discover as by study or inquiry. When applied to an object in the world—as Stein uses it here in "A Seltzer Bottle," from *Tender Buttons*—then "suppose" seems to discover the artefact in its minute distinction. And at the same time, being repeated and varied ("suppose" and "supposing") the word flies away from the fixity of objects, into a realm of elusive abstraction. It is exactly what I want from a sentence, this combination of oblique self-involvement and utter commitment to the things themselves. For words are also things and things are apt to burst with force and loud report.

How How How What What What How—When

"Considering how common illness is, how tremendous the spiritual change that it brings, how astonishing, when the lights of health go down, the undiscovered countries that are then disclosed, what wastes and deserts of the soul a slight attack of influenza brings to light, what precipices and lawns sprinkled with bright flowers a little rise of temperature reveals, what ancient and obdurate oaks are uprooted in us in the act of sickness, how we go down into the pit of death and feel the waters of annihilation close above our heads and wake thinking to find ourselves in the presence of the angels and the harpers when we have a tooth out and come to the surface in the dentist's arm chair and confuse his 'Rinse the mouth—rinse the mouth' with the greeting of the Deity stooping from the floor of Heaven to welcome us—when we think of this and infinitely more, as we are so frequently forced to think of it, it becomes strange indeed that illness has not taken its place with love, battle, and jealousy among the prime themes of literature."

—Virginia Woolf

IT MAY WELL BE the sentence that for diverse reasons—because thinking about Woolf, or sickness, or essays, because trying to emulate a certain rhythm in my own writing—I've copied out by hand more than any other. Each time, I've marvelled at the logic and ease and length (181 words) of the sentence, the hard clausal steps that slowly mount (or is it descend?) to a grammatically wrong-footing conclusion—the dash's flat fall where we might have expected a "then..." or "so..." I have wondered about the oddity of Woolf's metaphors—the sentence is mostly made of metaphors—and their unabashed mixture: the lights go up, the lights go down, the patient rises and falls as though in a rickety old elevator, till at last the cage clatters open, slightly missing the floor one wanted. This is the first sentence of Woolf's 1926 essay "On Being Ill," and it's hard to think of a verbal array whose structure better mimics both its subject and the larger text of which it's part: precisely because, despite its exquisitely shaped adventure, the sentence finally fails to hold itself together.

Everything that rises must converge, or not. Seven times—four hows and three whats—the sentence invites us to anticipate a logically and artistically satisfying terminus. With the final "how" we may reasonably expect that the grammatical, argumentative, and symbolic denouement is just around the comma-swivelling corner. Instead, we embark on a mysterious paratactic excursion, with no punctuation and no hint, for what seems an age, that our destination is the dentist's chair:

"we go down … and feel … and wake … and come to the surface … and confuse …" Everything tends towards the sentence's second and final dash—the first dash, the dentist's, may as well be any instrument at all—and an abrupt meta-swerve: "—when we think of this …" Do we, does even Woolf, really think of *this*? The sentence has allured us a long way, but I'm not certain I follow, not even sure what "this" consists of, never mind the "infinitely more."

Woolf was complexly unwell in the autumn of 1925, when T. S. Eliot asked if he might publish a piece of hers in the literary magazine *The Criterion*, which he had founded in 1922. (By the time Woolf's essay appeared, the journal had relaunched as *The New Criterion*.) The novelist was trying to start work on *To the Lighthouse*, but had been laid low by flu, headaches, and a vulturous pecking at the spine: this last, in a letter to her friend and lover Vita Sackville-West, is Woolf's way of describing her most recent mental and emotional breakdown. When she speaks in "On Being Ill" about "the act of sickness" (how odd, to think of it as an act) and "the great experience," when she imagines the moment when "we cease to be soldiers in the army of the upright," one may assume she has more vicious symptoms in mind than feebling coughs and sniffles. The essay is a lurid reflection on the uses of melancholy, the limits of sympathy, and the triumph of death.

You can hear in the delaying rhythms of the opening sentence the influence of Marcel Proust and the digressive, paid-by-the-word style of Thomas De Quincey, whose essays Woolf had lately written about in "Impassioned Prose." The asthmatic novelist and the opium-eating essayist are among the very few writers in whom, she tells us on the first page, we will find the subject of illness authoritatively or even adequately treated—"literature does its best to maintain that its concern is with the mind; that the body is a sheet of plain glass through which the soul looks straight and clear, and, save for one or two passions such as desire and greed, is null, negligible and nonexistent." We lack a language to capture "this monster, the body, this miracle, its pain," and if we tried to coin new words for the shiver and the headache, taking "pain in one hand and a lump of pure sound in the other," the result would likely be laughable. Only poets come close. So what would a prose literature devoted to illness sound like? Perhaps it could only exist in the form of the essay, of which genre Woolf's opening sentence is both an elegant part-for-whole and a less than obvious parody.

Woolf herself was ambivalent about "On Being Ill," and about its opening sentence. At first she and her husband Leonard Woolf thought the essay one of her best: it is funny, learned, vagrant, strange, and quite aware of the Montaigne-mimicking cliché of its titular "On . . ." Woolf was late sending it to Eliot, informing him, as the deadline passed, that the manuscript was imminent but she had been "working under difficulties." Eliot was willing to publish, but had reservations. His postcard to that effect has not survived; instead we have Woolf's letters and diaries, in which she laments that she may have overwritten. Returning to the text in light of Eliot's note, she "saw wordiness, feebleness, and all the vices in it." She had composed the essay from her sickbed, and it seemed that one of the main arguments of the piece—that the hiatus and the solitude of illness encourage a febrile sort of reading, and writing—had proved correct: Woolf had simply used too many words.

Four years after it first appeared, Woolf reprinted "On Being Ill" as part of a series of essay-length books for the Hogarth Press, which she had set up with Leonard. She took the opportunity to rein in what must have seemed syntactic and figural excesses in the work. In a passage about the invalid's attitude to poetry, the 1930 version states: "We rifle the poets of their flowers. We break off a line or two and let them open in the depths of the mind." But in 1926, Woolf had let the second prose flower bloom: "We break off a line or two and let them open in the depths of the mind, spread their bright wings, swim like coloured fish in green waters." Time and again in 1930, she strips away such decor: images disappear, adjectives vanish, and sentences quite as long as the opening one are pruned at their extremities as if they were rangy roses in her Sussex garden. The excess clauses are sometimes replanted or grafted nearby, not disposed of entirely.

There's a contradiction, not quite buried, in the way the essay characterizes the sick person's experience of language.

85

On the one hand: "Illness makes us disinclined for the long campaigns that prose exacts." The works of Edward Gibbon, Gustave Flaubert, and Henry James are beyond the powers of the bedridden, whose memory, judgement, and attention are apt to stray "while chapter swings on top of chapter." On the other hand, illness makes us adventurers, in language and imagination; we are pleased to abandon concision and coherence. Above all, so it seems as "On Being Ill" starts to mimic the shape of its own beginning, illness frees us to fall back on the pillows and give up pretending to the logical progression of our thoughts.

Here is what happens in 1930 to the first sentence of 1926: very little, almost nothing. There are some small changes to punctuation, as when "arm chair" acquires a hyphen. In a sentence that is governed in its opening lines by the (somewhat confusing) play of light and dark, Woolf avoids a minor repetition when she writes "what wastes and deserts of the soul a slight attack of influenza brings to view" instead of ". . . brings to light." Perhaps that change diverts the metaphoric force of the sentence a touch, but we are, after all, still in the territory of the visible, inside a reverie that with its field of flowers and "Deity stooping from the floor of Heaven" could be straight out of a medieval dream poem. The real alteration from the version of the sentence in *The New Criterion* comes a little way after the dash, when "and infinitely more" is quietly forgotten. It's hard not to conclude that Woolf's "infinitely more" is just this: the swelling perplex of metaphors, which she is doing her best to soothe and shrink.

What remains? Most of the sentence, and of course the crucial dash, which is the sveltest emblem possible of the license afforded to the sick, to the essayist, and to the sentence itself. "On Being Ill" contains one of Woolf's boldest essayistic deviations. She has been thinking about *Hamlet*, and the way rashness, "one of the properties of illness," allows at last a proper, because "outlaw," reading of the play's illogic and excess. And then, without warning: "But enough of Shakespeare—let us turn to Augustus Hare." Hare was a mediocre nineteenth-century biographer: his 1893 book *The Story of Two Noble Lives* (on Countess Canning and the Marchioness of Waterford) is the sort of thing one might have read in bed with flu in 1925. But it gives Woolf her last, long paragraph, on the eruption of violent death into poised, aristocratic Victorian lives. The essay ends in a kind of dream—with the image of a plush red curtain clasped and crushed in grief. And we're happy to follow Woolf there, in part, because of that dash in her opening sentence, which denotes a passage from the dream-fugue of sickness, depression, and undirected reading into the dirigible madness of writing.

All Kinds of Obscure Tensions

"What was important was not our having penicillin when they had none, nor the unregarding munificence of the French Ministry of Reconstruction (as it was then called), but the occasional glimpse obtained, by us in them and also, who knows, by them in us (for they are an imaginative people), of that smile at the human condition as little to be extinguished by bombs as to be broadened by the elixirs of Burroughes and Welcome,—the smile deriding, among other things, the having and the not having, the giving and the taking, sickness and health."

—SAMUEL BECKETT

BUT FIRST, another sentence, from one of the few passages in Beckett that I can recite accurately from memory; many others have stuck less fast in the mind for decades, and all will bring on a genuine shiver when read, or heard in the theatre. "The way they went down, sighing before the stem!" It is from *Krapp's Last Tape*, and the exclamation mark is Beckett's. Alone on stage, the elderly Krapp listens to recordings of his younger self, or rather selves. The frail bit of memory at the heart of the play is a moment, told first in a fragment and then heard in full, when Krapp as a young man lies in a punt, on a lake, with his lover, on the verge of ending their relationship. "I said again that I thought it was hopeless and no good going on, and she agreed, without opening her eyes." The girl, with her green eyes and green coat, is based on Beckett's cousin Peggy Sinclair, with whom he'd had a brief romance at the end of the 1920s. Here is more of the passage:

> I asked her to look at me and after a few moments—(*pause*)—after a few moments she did, but the eyes just slits, because of the glare. I bent over her to get them in the shadow and they opened. (*Pause. Low.*) Let me in. (*Pause.*) We drifted in among the flags and stuck. The way they went down, sighing before the stem! (*Pause.*) I lay down across her with my face in her breasts and my hand on her. We lay there without moving. But under us all moved, and moved us, gently, up and down, and from side to side.

There are equally, perhaps even more, beautiful stretches of prose in Beckett's novels and stories and plays, moments in the latter reaches of *Not I* or *Rockaby*, or in the shrinking late fiction, that possess a more abstracted aesthetic chill, or intellectual thrill. (Hugh Kenner: "I could show you a Beckett sentence

89

as elegant in its implications as the binomial theorem, and another as economically sphynx-like as the square root of minus one, and another, on trees in the night, for which half of Wordsworth would seem a fair exchange.") The start of *Company*, for example, with its echo of Saint Augustine, which I think of frequently: "A voice comes to one in the dark. Imagine. To one on his back in the dark." But it is hard to think of a more completely lyrical series of sentences than these from *Krapp's Last Tape*. Just listen to the sound of it again, the repeated "w" and "s"—"The way they went down, sighing before the stem!" And the ambiguity of "stem," which is an obsolete name for the timber at, or the whole extremity of, the prow or stern of a vessel. But "stem" also makes us think of the stems of the "flags," that is *Acorus calamus*, the lakeside plants into which the punt has drifted. I am not ashamed to say that each time I've seen the play performed, there have been tears when Krapp reaches this line. And I'm not sure that the alliteration and the semantic quibble of *stem* have not moved me as much as the scene these sentences describe, with its vision of a love lost to time and the awful downward drag of regret. The sort of sentence, then, that you would be mad not to want to write about. But something urges me away from it: the lyric perfection of the thing, schooled on James Joyce, which neither Krapp nor Beckett wishes us to accept without suspicion. The desperate, moving brilliance of the sentence, of the scene, is not only internal; it's also in the fact that this moment is caught up in Krapp's retrospective self-loathing and Beckett's own merciless efforts to rid himself of Joyce's influence. The sentence is not what it seems, nor how it sounds, but is raddled with irony. Still, its sentiment survives all that.

Start again, another sentence of Beckett's that I cannot ignore, even if this one, also, I cannot recite.

> What was important was not our having penicillin when they had none, nor the unregarding munificence of the French Ministry of Reconstruction (as it was then called), but the occasional glimpse obtained, by us in them and also, who knows, by them in us (for they are an imaginative people), of that smile at the human condition as little to be extinguished by bombs as to be broadened by the elixirs of Burroughes and Welcome,— the smile deriding, among other things, the having and the not having, the giving and the taking, sickness and health.

I have in front of me on my desk a small booklet of postcards with a crumbling brown cover and a diagonally printed title: "Saint-Lô, Capitale des Ruines, 5 et 7 juin 1944." Saint-Lô is a city in Normandy, capital of the Manche and after Cherbourg the second largest city in the department. During the Second World War, Saint-Lô became an organizational centre and transport hub for the German army, and when the Allies invaded in June 1944, the town found itself directly south of two D-Day landing points, the beaches named Utah and

Omaha. On the 6th of June, American planes began attacking Saint-Lô, killing 800 people on the first night and levelling most buildings in the city.

The postcards show Saint-Lô before and after it was bombed, starting with a general view of the pre-war city across the river Vire, with the church of Notre-Dame de Saint-Lô in the upper left, rising over bristling rooftops and trees. On the second postcard, there are perhaps a couple of roofs and gables still intact, most of the buildings have vanished, the trees are a few needling black Giacometti stumps, and the cathedral looks untouched (it was not). Here is the sunlit Hôtel de Ville: the tall door half open, three floors of classical columns and curtained windows, surmounted by a clock—it is almost eleven in the morning. And over the page the same building: the roof gone and with it the clock, while the upper windows open onto daylight. The blackened facade looks ashamed of itself. Pre-war Notre-Dame, with its own off-centre clock, its placid environs empty but for three tiny figures—then in 1944 it's as if the church, half standing, has vomited into the Place Notre-Dame and towards the camera, disgorging more rubble than the building could possibly contain. Streets and squares no longer streets or squares, everything empty and pale and reduced to fragments you could hold in your hand. It looks like any other bombed-out town or city of the war, all of its particulars now turned abstract. About Saint-Lô, people said that even the rubble was rubble.

Beckett arrived in Saint-Lô in August 1945. During the war, he had risked his life for the Resistance, then fled Paris for Roussillon, in the Vaucluse, where he had a breakdown, but began work on his novel *Watt*. After the Liberation, he travelled to London and on to Dublin, where he was effectively stranded until he joined the staff of a Red Cross hospital that was planned for Saint-Lô. When he got there, he wrote to a friend, Thomas MacGreevy:

> St. Lô is just a heap of rubble, La Capitale des Ruines as they call it in France. Of 2600 buildings 2000 completely wiped out, 400 badly damaged and 200 'only' slightly.... It has been raining hard the last few days and the place is a sea of mud. What it will be like in winter is hard to imagine. No lodging of course of any kind.

There were, he told MacGreevy, "all kinds of obscure tensions" between "the local medical crowd" and the Red Cross. In his role of storekeeper-interpreter Beckett worked seven days a week, and was frequently employed as a driver, picking up new doctors and nurses from the port of Dieppe, one hundred and sixty miles away. By all accounts he was well liked by his colleagues; he was a "free thinker," but genial and kind towards these pious men and women who had never been outside Ireland before.

"The Capital of the Ruins" is a short essay or report about

his time in Saint-Lô that it seems Beckett wrote in 1946 for Radio Éireann, as the Irish state broadcaster was then known. The piece lay unknown until 1983, when it was discovered in the RTE archives. Three years later it was published in *The Beckett Country*, Eoin O'Brien's richly illustrated book about Beckett and Ireland. In the same year, "The Capital of the Ruins" appeared, on the occasion of Beckett's eightieth birthday, in John Calder's anthology *As No Other Dare Fail*. There, it was said to have been read by Beckett himself on radio, on the 10th of June 1946. In fact no evidence exists that it was ever broadcast. It is not at all surprising however that the radio station and an Irish audience would have been interested in what he had to say—not because it was Beckett, whose writings were hardly known, but because the Irish hospital at Saint-Lô, and the experiences of those who had gone to work there, were already in the news. The hospital's director, Colonel Thomas McKinney, had described on radio a city that "may be described as 100 per cent flattened—the work of a few hours from the air." It had been suggested in the press that the efforts of the Irish staff had gone unappreciated in France; Beckett's text is not exactly a corrective, but an oddly toned description of the complexities involved.

He begins in a descriptive style, setting a scene in the conventional fashion of radio reportage. "On what a year ago was a grassy slope, lying in the angle that the Vire and the Bayeux roads make as they unite at the entrance of the town, opposite

what remains of the second most important stud-farm in
France, a general hospital now stands." There are twenty-five
prefab huts, insulated with fibreglass and panelled in Isorel or
masonite. The hospital's operating theatre is lined with aero-
nautic aluminium: "a decorative and practical solution of an
old problem and a pleasant variation on the sword and plough-
share metamorphosis." There is a laboratory where "considerable work has already been done in the analysis of local waters."
Covered passageways connect wards and refectories; the complex is provided with central heating and electric light. (Is there
a reminder of Beckett's account of the hospital layout in a
fiction like *The Lost Ones*, with its detailing of a grey-lit rotunda
and its half-living denizens?) The hospital, says Beckett, treats
ninety in-patients at a time, and up to 200 out-patients each
day. There are the usual problems of the bombed-out and
homeless, such as scabies and malnutrition, also accidental
injuries: "Masonry falls when least expected, children play with
detonators and demining continues."

The essay carries on in this reportorial vein for a while, and
then something curious happens to "The Capital of the Ruins."
The preceding descriptions, Beckett says, were suited to certain
medically minded listeners:

These are the sensible people who would rather have news of
the Norman's semicircular canals or resistance to sulphur than
of his attitude to the Irish bringing gifts, who would prefer the

history of our difficulties with an unfamiliar pharmacopoeia and system of mensuration to the story of our dealings with the rare and famous ways of spirit that are the French ways.

If there have been tensions between the Irish and the French, they have not been to do with differences of opinion or expectation regarding medical treatment, but rather differences of emotional outlook. Here is what happens either side of the sentence:

And yet the whole enterprise turned from the beginning on the establishing of a relation in the light of which the therapeutic relation faded to the merest of pretexts. What was important was not our having penicillin when they had none, nor the unregarding munificence of the French Ministry of Reconstruction (as it was then called), but the occasional glimpse obtained, by us in them and also, who knows, by them in us (for they are an imaginative people), of that smile at the human condition as little to be extinguished by bombs as to be broadened by the elixirs of Burroughes and Welcome,—the smile deriding, among other things, the having and the not having, the giving and the taking, sickness and health.

It would not be seemly, in a retiring and indeed retired storekeeper, to describe the obstacles encountered in this connexion, and the forms, often grotesque, devised for them by the combined energies of the home and visiting temperaments. It must be supposed that they were not insurmountable, since they have long ceased to be of much account. When I reflect now on the recurrent problems of what, with all proper modesty, might be called the heroic period, on one in particular so arduous and elusive that it literally ceased to be formulable, I suspect that our pains were those inherent in the simple and necessary and yet so unattainable proposition that their way of being we, was not our way and that our way of being they, was not their way. It is only fair to say that many of us had never been abroad before.

This may all seem a laboured and roundabout way of saying that the French and Irish differed in temperament. "A retiring and indeed retired storekeeper." It is possible to regret the tone of lofty self-deprecation that pervades this passage. ("Pervades" is an awful word: something of Beckett's pomposity is catching.) As well as, perhaps, his elaborate reticence on some matters—what, for instance, was the problem "so arduous and elusive that it literally ceased to be formulable"? By contrast, the long sentence in the first of these paragraphs is a monument to clarification, a sort of syntactic Hôtel de Ville with bombed-out windows for clauses, each framing a little too starkly the harsh history behind this sober edifice.

In its stiff dance of qualifications and parentheses, it sounds more like Henry James than James Joyce. "Nor," "but," "also": a kind of sifting is going on in the first half, an organization

97

and elucidation that sounds very fitting for a "storekeeper-interpreter." Beckett seems to be reaching for a literary, essayistic style, or parodying same, much in the manner that *Watt* does, with its endless pedantic descriptions of Watt's way of walking or his daily regime for feeding scraps to Mr. Knott's dog. The parentheses seem excessive—does it matter to the Irish audience what exactly the ministry was called? (It was *Le ministère de la Reconstruction et de l'Urbanisme.*) Can we not imagine that the French may be imaginative enough to imagine how the Irish imagine their shared circumstance? Do we need to be told "they are an imaginative people"? And isn't there something awkward about those gerunds towards the end— "the having and the not having, the giving and the taking"? Or a little too balanced about "as little to be extinguished" and "as to be broadened"? (By the way, Beckett has misspelled both *Burroughs* and *Wellcome.*) I have the impression, however, that all of this syntactical and grammatical *business*—akin to the fiddling with hats and boots and spools of tape in his plays—is somehow necessary to the expression of a harsh but heartening truth: there was a cold sort of humour to be found in Saint-Lô.

I'm not the first to light on this sentence and wonder at its peculiar shape and tone. Two of Beckett's acutest readers have done the same, and come to very different conclusions. In 1998 the scholar and critic Steven Connor reviewed biographies of Beckett by James Knowlson and Anthony Cronin, and remarked on the "shocking frigidity" of "The Capital of the

Ruins," which he takes as an example of the immature writer's self-regard, and his inability fully to sympathize with the bombed-out populace. Quoting this sentence—and from the essay, only this sentence—Connor writes:

> Only a knowledge of the humanity of Beckett's later explorations of the inhuman condition could rescue the insufferable, sarky high-mindedness of stuff like this. . . . The most emphatic sign of humanisation in the writing that Beckett was already doing in *Watt* by this time would be the ethical dilapidations it wrought (not least with the meddling power of the comma) on the stifled, self-regarding composure of sentences like the above.

I can quite see what Connor means. And yet, here is the philosopher Simon Critchley, latching on to the same sentence at the end of his 2002 book *On Humour*: "For me, it is this smile—deriding the having and the not having, the pleasure and the pain, the sublimity and suffering of the human situation—that is the essence of humour." The smile that passes obscurely between the French and the Irish at Saint-Lô is "the laugh of laughs, the *risus purus*, the laugh laughing at the laugh": a lucid, melancholy, consoling laughter, which is all we have at the last.

(Small Pictures 1915–1940)

"His constant nagging at the attention by petty and often vapid titles is a sign of his own nervousness and of a documentation which is perhaps too thorough; he had made himself too accessible."

—FRANK O'HARA

THE VERY FIRST THINGS I wrote professionally were 300-word book reviews for *Time Out* magazine in London. I thought then, twenty years ago, and sometimes think fondly now, that I could happily do that job till the end of my days, and never tire of its rigours or wish for a longer word count. The constraint of the task taught me how to write, which I took to mean, for better and worse, how to maximize style, thought and range of reference in a piece of writing that would end up, on the printed page, about the size of a bus ticket. I frequently scanted, to say the least, the plots or arguments of the books I was writing about. But I have hardly ever felt so pleased as a writer as when I had pared my piece to precisely 300 words, never more or less.

The exhibition review from which I've extracted this sentence is only 207 words long. It is March 1954, and O'Hara, a prolific critic as well as poet, is writing in *Art News* about Paul Klee, fourteen years after the artist's death. As in many of O'Hara's reviews, he hardly pauses to tell us, at least in any literal fashion, what the work in the exhibition actually looks like. He seems instead, in every sentence, to crystallize something in the art or the artist. About Klee, his opening could be a description of O'Hara's critical style: "Paul Klee is fortunate in never having done a major work; each individual thought as it comes to us trembling with wit and sensibility seems to be all of him. Almost."

One longs in Klee's art, says O'Hara, for the one great sustained statement; but instead we have these beguiling minor works, which have come together like errant children for an anniversary party. "When they go away again they will be individuals, but for now their family resemblance is very strong. Some of them are beautiful and amusing, others are phlegmatic and puerile." Perhaps it seems trifling of O'Hara, in his final sentence, to criticize Klee for the whimsicality of his titles. But the point turns so swiftly, so delicately, into a sympathetic diagnosis of Klee's fretful efforts to control the reception of his art. You don't have to agree with O'Hara to appreciate the brilliance and pathos of his turn to the pluperfect in the last clause: "he had made himself too accessible." And more: if readers of *Art News* were paying attention, they might have heard in those summative words a poetic echo of W. H. Auden, in 1939, writing about the death of W. B. Yeats: "The current of his feeling failed; he became his admirers."

Splinters of Actuality

"Speed sublimates, melting repetitive advertisements, gargantuan trios of tin red roses, black griffins rampant on yellow banners, into fluid ribbons, also unweaving skylines, liquefying stoniness into lakes, powdering changing heights with more and more unattainable little towns like sun-splashes."

—Elizabeth Bowen

FOR MORE THAN HALF MY LIFE I have been failing to read Elizabeth Bowen. Aged nineteen, at university, I was supposed to study *The Last September*, but whether from adolescent antipathy to the lectures on what was then still called "Anglo-Irish literature," or from some allergy to the milieu of the "Big House" novel, I'm quite sure I never bought the book, let alone read it. Actually, it cannot have been for the second reason: I felt no such animus (except when it came to Waugh and Catholicism) towards *Brideshead Revisited*, and I remember in the summer of 1986, when I was seventeen, borrowing one of my father's Molly Keane novels, then recently republished by Virago. I recall only the grand and threatened Edwardian setting, and I think the book must have been *The Rising Tide*, from 1937. (The reason I cannot remember: I read it in a sort of stupor, trying not to think about the fact it was a year to the week since my mother died.) At the end of my first year of English at college, I started reading, and loving, *The Waves*, and maybe like a fool I thought I had found in Virginia Woolf a more exacting version of the exquisite modernism I'd been promised in *The Last September*.

An accidental reminder—in this case, a student's enthusiasm for the grace and strangeness of Elizabeth Bowen's sentences—and you can find yourself nursing an obsession with a writer you'd ignored, forgotten or kept at a guilty remove for decades. At this urgent exploratory stage, it is easy to be put off and easy to invest too much. I was afraid some pages-long stretch of dialogue might bore me and merely remind me of all the other books I could or should be reading, and so decided to start with Bowen's essays. As I write, I'm two thirds of the way through *A Time in Rome*, which she published in 1960, and I think I have found, again, a writer after my heart. How many times does it happen, dare it happen, in a life of reading? A dozen, maybe? There is a difference between the writers you can read and admire all your life, and the others, the voices for whom you feel some more intimate affinity. Could Elizabeth Bowen be turning swiftly into one of the latter, on account of her amazing sentences?

"Speed sublimates, melting repetitive advertisements, gargantuan trios of tin red roses, black griffins rampant on yellow banners, into fluid ribbons, also unweaving skylines, liquefying stoniness into lakes, powdering changing heights with more and more unattainable little towns like sun-splashes." In the passage where this sentence appears, Bowen is describing what it is like to drive, or be driven, on the outskirts of Rome. (There is a related sentence much later in the book, when she is describing Saint Paul's approach to Rome around AD 60: "Thickening in the distance, in the dust from chariots and dusk from gardens, began to materialize the city, trimmed with the topmost flashes of gilt spokes.") The sentence perfectly expresses the sleek blur of a sunlit road—but how does Bowen do it? In part, with a rush of impersonality: the agent here is speed itself, and not the wide-eyed passenger who feels its effects. "Sublimates" is ideal, bearing here its chemical, or alchemical, sense; the other verbs—"melting," "unweaving," "liquefying," "powdering"—are all variations on this one, efforts to define its undefining energy. The sentence is an appositive elaboration of its two-word opening clause, a fluid system that once set in motion may generate new clauses, new examples, new glances through the windscreen or the passenger window, for as long as the writer keeps calmly her foot on the accelerator. Strictly speaking the sentence is a potentially infinite branching of new qualifying clauses, but the effect instead is a sliding from one to another, a cinematic sweep, a zoom and pan rather than montage of views. (Bowen, in her

"Notes on Writing a Novel," in 1945: "The cinema, with its actual camera-work, is interesting study for the novelist.")

It is early in my adventure with Bowen's prose, but already there are features of a sentence like this one that capture the ear and eye. Hard not to admire the compact soundscape of certain phrases: "trios of tin red roses...fluid ribbons." But also the (presumably) deliberate infelicity of "powdering changing heights"—and isn't this also a slightly confusing phrase, the powdering not fitting as well as we might hope with the splashing at the end of the sentence? As for "stoniness": Bowen has a habit of naming qualities in this fashion, even when it leads to obvious awkwardnesses. Here she is, fifty pages later, describing some of Rome's looming ruins: "On the Forum side, the built-up Hill of the Caesars looks like a giant derelict hotel: a honeycomb of arches of keyhole narrowness, cavernous windows, gloomy vaulted apartments, ramps, and galleries. The overhangingness and the staringness are unnerving." "Overhangingness" and "staringness": these are words at which many editors would flinch. And it seems that Bowen's publishers did baulk at times when presented with her more perverse word choices and contrary phrase-making. In 1948 she sent the manuscript of her novel *The Heat of the Day* to her London publisher Jonathan Cape, and received in reply a somewhat troubled reader's report: "Generally I notice the phrase 'could but' is overworked and so is the trick of double negatives." Bowen, said the report, sometimes "abused" style, to the "reader's discomfort," and wrote a prose "more Jacobean than James." But Bowen knew exactly what she was doing: "I'd rather keep the jars 'jangles' and awkwardnesses—e.g. 'seemed unseemly', 'felt to falter'. They do to my mind express something. In some cases I want the rhythm to jerk or jar—to an extent, even, which may displease the reader." Note, even here, the awkwardness of "awkwardnesses."

In *A Time in Rome*, the jars and jangles contend with, or subvert, a prose that is otherwise calm and elegant and vividly imagistic. On the Basilica Sotterranea: "One thinks of a cathedral at the bottom of the sea, but that the building is pagan, the sea is earth, unmurmuringly pressing against the walls." I have a feeling that Jonathan Cape's anonymous reader would not have cared for "but that," still less for the adverb "unmurmuringly." But these are the sorts of details that have already drawn me in to Bowen's style, made me both regret my youthful ignorance and thank my callow self for giving me in middle age the belated gift of this prose, which is neither as poised and detached as thirty years ago I imagined it would be, nor as opaque and mannered as is sometimes said. It is a style by turns exact, easeful and bristling.

Obeying the Form of the Curve

"They thought he was a real sweet ofay cat,
but a little frantic."

—JAMES BALDWIN

IN 1956, IN THE *Village Voice*, where for four months he contributed a regular column, Norman Mailer published "The Hip and the Square": an account of two competing styles of being—cultural, political, racial, spiritual and bodily—whose contemporary juxtaposition came down for Mailer, at least at this moment, to a rather crude face-off between two lists. Among the terms belonging in the domain of the hip: *wild, romantic, intuit, Negro, inductive, nihilistic, associative, obeying the form of the curve.* And on the other side: *practical, classic, logic, white, programmatic, authoritarian, sequential, living in the cell of the square.* The following year, in his essay "The White Negro," Mailer enlarged on the definition of hip: though the word was not his, he badly wished to own it, and to inhabit it, to be hip. In "The White Negro," with its scattershot sense of where the new (actually, not so new) sensibility lives in the American scene—amid jazz, drugs, sex, violence and a literary turn with which Mailer would like to be associated—to be hip is above all to be black, male and sexually potent.

Mailer included "The White Negro" in his 1959 essay collection *Advertisements for Myself*. Also in that book was a piece called "Evaluations—Quick and Expensive Comments on Some Talent in the Room," in which Mailer passed judgement on his contemporaries. Among them was James Baldwin, whom he called "too charming to be major." "Charming" is a way of signalling but not saying that Baldwin was gay—it is not quite so blatant as the claim that "even the best of his paragraphs is sprayed with perfume." In an ecstasy of bad faith, Mailer concludes that Baldwin's problem is that he's "incapable of saying 'F— you' to the reader."

Baldwin thought of disabusing Mailer of this last belief—at least in so far as it applied to one reader—by sending his sometime friend a telegram straight away. Instead Baldwin waited, and when in 1961 he published "The Black Boy Looks at the White Boy," it was not only a response to Mailer's boorish comments about his fiction, but also a comprehensive trashing of the white writer's attitudes to black male sexuality—and of his efforts to mimic the same. Baldwin and Mailer had met in Paris. Mailer may have been the more successful writer, but Baldwin is keen to establish that he was himself not without presence, or ego: "I was then (and I have not changed much) a very tight, tense, lean, abnormally ambitious, abnormally intelligent, and hungry black cat." Baldwin had spent many evenings with Mailer and his wife Adele Morales, and had begun to feel that here was a friend, that a real warmth existed between them.

Still, it seemed to Baldwin that Mailer laboured under certain delusions, which it was the unwanted task of his new black friend to bolster. In common with other contemporary white writers like Jack Kerouac, Mailer had come to believe in a sexualized mystique surrounding black masculinity, which in literature—and perhaps as ruinously in life—he hoped to match. It had, Baldwin contended, nothing at all to do with real black experience. Though of course there *was* a violent black masculinity, and Baldwin had suffered its brutality, as he had suffered from the violence of white power. He was in no mind to accept the sentimental vision of "The White Negro": Baldwin bristled at the very title, and felt "a kind of fury that so antique a vision of the blacks should, at this late hour, and in so many borrowed heirlooms, be stepping off the A train."

In Paris, Mailer's romantic view of black experience had been obvious to Baldwin, but he had not felt able to correct it:

And matters were not helped at all by the fact that the Negro jazz musicians, among whom we sometimes found ourselves, who really liked Norman, did not for an instant consider him as being even remotely "hip" and Norman did not know this and I could not tell him. He never broke through to them, at least as far as I know; and they were far too "hip," if that is the word I want, even to consider breaking through to him. They thought he was a real sweet ofay cat, but a little frantic.

"If that is the word I want": Baldwin is making a slight show here of being careful with his language, coolly implying a distinction between Mailer's (and a larger white culture's) slack use of "hip" to appropriate the perceived liberties of African-American art or life, and the stricter sense the word maintained among black people themselves. To be hip and black at mid-century meant, for sure, to inhabit the sort of peripheral milieu—of style and sex, of drugs, art and crime—to which Mailer in his half-invented innocence was attracted. But the "benediction of hip" (as the critic Ian Penman calls it) also implies a type of reserve, remoteness, austerity. Hip is a matter of codes and ciphers, hidden meanings—because the alternative, in the lethal perplex of race in America, is literally to give yourself away. This is what the garrulous Mailer cannot grasp.

"They thought he was a real sweet ofay cat, but a little frantic." In its smooth way, it is the most damning putdown of Mailer in the whole essay. The mostly monosyllabic rhythms of the sentence and its neatly affianced sounds ("real sweet," "ofay cat" and "frantic") are Baldwin's, but they belong also to the jazz musicians he is half quoting. The sentence is an example of what is clumsily called *free indirect speech*: the author sounding like subject or character. It is straightforwardly comical too: hard not to think literally of Mailer as "a frantic cat." But something else interests me in the sentence: Baldwin's use of the word "ofay," which has a fraught and fascinating history. Superficially, it simply means white: that is, if you are African-American and intending by the word a certain degree of contempt, offence or dismissal. Quite how much hostility it expresses seems to have varied with geography and history, during a century and more of use. "Ofay" did not reach mainstream white America in the way, for example, that "honky" did—though there is some evidence to say that in parts of the United States it was the more violent epithet.

But why "ofay"? If you google the word now you will find some more or less exotic etymologies. It is said to be a Pig Latin version of "foe." Or, as the *Dictionary of American Regional English* suggests, to derive from the Ibibio language of Nigeria. (Claims of African origin have also been made for "hip," which dates in English at least to 1904—these seem to be fanciful.) But another origin suggests itself for "ofay," and a history that haunts Baldwin's use of the word, which appears to me both casual and considered. The linguist Gerald Cohen has proposed that the word is a corruption of "au fait," which was in wide use in the US by the end of the nineteenth century to mean fashionable, knowing, particular. "Au fait" appears to have migrated to mean, among black Americans, a particular sort of white person or white culture: middle-class, condescending, excessively correct. And from there simply to mean white. In the early decades of the twentieth century, for example, the word was in regular use at a prominent black newspaper, the *Baltimore Afro-American*, where a reporter or, as in this case, the author of a letter, might feel the need to explain: "I think it would be a good idea to warn our people through your publication of this Northern ofay's (so-called white) boast how easily he is getting rich off the profits to be made from our people." The word did not, it seems, penetrate the whole community. In 1931 a black reader wrote to the *Afro-American*: "I want you to explain the meaning of the term 'ofay', which I see so often in your valued paper. Is it used in a good sense or does it carry with it some shame?" To which the editors replied: "This reader flies to conclusions which are not justified. No antagonism is expressed in the word ofay (originally au fait), applied to white people, any more than there is in the word sepia, applied to coloured folk." The comparison with "sepia" points to another antique term, and perhaps casts some doubt on the claim that "ofay" is used quite neutrally. (On the other hand, *Sepia* was later the title of a magazine, aimed at African-American readers, that was published in Fort Worth, Texas, from 1947 to 1983.) Here is "ofay" hovering between mainstream and specialist or elite use, and revealing at the same time its likely origin in "au fait."

All of this is present in Baldwin's use of the word, but he is also being more exact than this brief etymological excursion allows. "Ofay" is especially weighted or inflected in the context of jazz, in the context of hip, where it's possible to speak of an ofay crowd, an ofay audience, as the citizens of a beautiful and too-much-visited city might speak of tourists. Billie Holiday, in her 1956 autobiography, *Lady Sings the Blues*: "Most of the ofays, the white people, who came to Harlem those nights were looking for atmosphere." "Ofay" signals a point of contact, a scene of expectation, voyeurism, performance and judgement. And it carries with it some recollection of its French original, or rather the Anglophone iteration of "au fait." This is Duke Ellington, in his 1973 autobiography, *Music Is My Mistress*: "When I first went to Europe on the Olympic in 1933, I felt so au fait with all that silverware on the table."

A paradox in Baldwin's use of the term: if "ofay" describes a particular kind of white desire to condescend and become otherwise, to inhabit Afro-American culture, if only as hipster spectator, then it comes oddly close to the ambiguity of "hip" itself. Both words contain versions of rectitude and liberty. (The first uses of "hip" in the early twentieth century, so an OED editor Jessie Sheidlower has argued, suggest precisely "in the know" or "aware.") But here is the larger binary with which Baldwin is working in this sentence: if "ofay" is in most senses the opposite of "hip," then "frantic" is assuredly the anti-pode of an absent term, "cool." And cool, for all its connotations of ease and swagger, is also a matter of control. Mailer's problem is not quite that he cannot contain himself; rather, that he aspires so cravenly to a state of liberation that does not really exist, let alone for the black men in whom he thinks he has seen it. In the end, for Baldwin, the cult of hip misunderstood, the veneration of a caricature of black masculinity, the ambition to face down American power without ever having to experience its real depredations—all this, Baldwin writes, is "a way of avoiding all of the terrors of life and love."

The Grand Illusion

"Opposite, above: All through the house, colour, verve, improvised treasures in happy but anomalous coexistence."

—JOAN DIDION

I AM ONE OF THOSE readers of magazines and journals who turn to the list of contributors before the table of contents; I want to know who before I know what. Often, the writers will have been asked to supply little biographical notices of themselves—these may tend to whimsy, or self-regard—so that even if I don't know their work already, I can guess what sort of voice they will have on the page. Reading online, a comparable thing may happen, the social-media reputation preceding the text you might otherwise have missed. *I wrote about X . . . Here's a piece by Y.* It is easy to forget how much periodical writing of the past was originally anonymous. Many of Virginia Woolf's best critical essays, for example, were published anonymously in the *Times Literary Supplement*. But at the *Times Lit* (as people called it then) nobody had a byline; the case is different for writers whose early or occasional work appeared uncredited alongside stories, essays and articles by prominently named authors. It is no surprise that in this category there are many women: the likes of Maeve Brennan, Jamaica Kincaid and Janet Malcolm, just to mention writers who quickened their art in the (then) mostly anonymizing front section of the *New Yorker*.

In the early 1960s, while on the staff of *Vogue*, Joan Didion was only half known to the magazine's readers. Her name appeared intermittently; her first signed piece, in June 1961, was a short essay on jealousy, which already showed certain features of her mature writing: an earnest consideration of the brittle contours of her own character, and a fine attention to language, including her own. "A passion for the documentation of irrelevant detail is characteristic of the afflicted"—of course, we are meant to understand, the detail is never irrelevant. The jealousy essay did not appear in her first collection, *Slouching Towards Bethlehem*; but just as in the celebrated writings in that book—on self-respect, on John Wayne, on keeping a note-book, on New York and its discontents—you can see, or hear, her becoming Joan Didion in "Jealousy: Is It a Curable Disease?" It takes more than the odd essay, however, to train yourself to the particular pitch that Didion did in those years. More too than sitting at her sturdy Royal and typing out hunks of Hemingway, by way of practice, as Didion insists she did.

What more, what else? She wrote short, unattributed paragraphs—they could not be called essays, articles or pieces—for

Vogue's regular "People Are Talking About" column. She wrote about *Dr. No* and *The Manchurian Candidate*; about the atom bomb, Telstar and the construction of the Guggenheim; on the budding careers of Willem de Kooning, Woody Allen and Barbara Streisand; and about the death of Marilyn Monroe, "a profoundly moving young woman." She also composed photo captions: those "signposts," as Walter Benjamin put it, that had become essential to the printed magazine page in the twentieth century. In *Vogue*, by the 1960s, captions were surprisingly substantial pieces of writing, and were accorded what might seem a remarkable amount of editorial care. The captions Didion wrote make up a minor, telling aspect of the mythology around her work. Perhaps "mythology" is the wrong word. It is a matter of style, where style is verifiable presence on the page, a question of materiality. Didion is frequently described as an exact and exacting writer, building her prose like a shiny carapace, easy to admire and hard to crack if you're hoping to emulate it. At the same time, she has a reputation for being, on the page and in person, brittle and neurasthenic, spectral and barely there. None of this adequately describes her prose. It is usually direct and declarative, it is filled with parallelisms and rhythmic repetitions, there is a wealth of concrete detail. Irony in her work consists largely of the plain statement of such detail, inflected by the innocent, mad or bad-faith language of the people or institutions she is writing about. Sometimes she leaves this plane for another, more abstracted or metaphorical, gothic even. As for instance this famous passage from "The White Album," in which she is describing the feeling of dread and coming disaster that prevailed in Los Angeles at the end of the 1960s: "A demented and seductive vortical tension was building in the community. The jitters were setting in. I recall a time when the dogs barked every night and the moon was always full." These sentences are followed by an extremely precise recollection of where she was, and with whom, at the moment she heard about the Manson murders. In a lecture at UCLA in 1971, Didion said: "I'm not much interested in spontaneity; I'm not an inspirational writer. What concerns me is total control."

Producing captions, Didion has said, was part of mounting "the monthly grand illusion" of a glossy magazine. The editor-in-chief then was Diana Vreeland, but the more detailed work was done by Allene Talmey, who had been with *Vogue* since the mid-1930s, and became associate editor in 1963. By the accounts of Didion and her contemporaries, Talmey was an unsparing editor and boss. After she had wielded her pencil on another writer's copy—tapping on the table all the while a large aquamarine and silver ring—the young woman was wrung out: "Well, my dear, I used to go home, sit in the tub and *weep*." Interviewed by the *Paris Review* in 1978, Didion said: "Every day I would go into [Talmey's] office with eight lines of copy or a caption or something. She would sit there and mark it up with a pencil and get very angry about extra words, about verbs not working." Didion was profiled by the *New York Times* in 1979, and in that piece Talmey herself told how she would ask Didion to write a caption of three or four hundred words, and together they would cut it down to fifty. "We wrote long and published short and by doing that Joan learned to write."

The *New York Times* article coincided with the publication of *Telling Stories*, Didion's only collection of short fiction—if you could call three stories a collection. In this book's preface, she enlarges on her time at *Vogue* and the rigours of working under Talmey. "We were connoisseurs of synonyms. We were collectors of verbs." Certain words went in and out of fashion: "to ravish" was for some months an editorially approved verb. "I also recall it, for a number of issues more, as the source of a highly favoured noun: 'ravishments', as in *tables cluttered with porcelain tulips, Fabergé eggs, other ravishments*." Didion and her young colleagues learned—"or one did not stay"—to use active verbs instead of passive, to make sure "it" always had a nearby reference, to reach for the OED to ensure surprise as much as precision. And most of all they learned to rewrite, time and again, in search of the correct balance of elegance and excitement. "Run it through again, sweetie," Talmey told them, "it's not quite there."

"Opposite, above: All through the house, colour, verve, improvised treasures in happy but anomalous coexistence." I came across the sentence first online, in the 1979 profile, where it is offered as an example of Didion's caption-writing for *Vogue* at the start of her career. So much to admire: not least, the verbless economy of the sentence, as if the caption's deictic function—its act of pointing, or its open-handed gesture—quite does away with the need for verbs. (What would the verbed alternatives be? "All through the house *are* colour, verve . . ." Or *there are.* Or *one finds.* The possible additions all seem to weaken the sentence.) There is some tension, isn't there, between "Opposite, above" and "All through the house"? Or perhaps not: the caption directs us to a single picture, but it stands for the whole. "All through the house": with its slumberous familiarity—"It was the night before Christmas . . ."—it conjures time as well as space. We're drifting or processing through this house (and we'll soon be able to say which house). In her preface to *Telling Stories*, Didion recalls that Talmey, following rhetorical fashion, likes things, especially qualifiers, to come in threes. And so it is here with the somewhat abstracted features of house and household—"colour, verve, improvised treasures." What *is* an improvised treasure? A found object, or Duchampian readymade, whose meaning or value derives from the artist-collector's choosing and acquiring it? Or maybe "improvised" refers to a casual or intuitive arrangement or mode of display, to a style of living with things rather than the things themselves?

"Happy but anomalous coexistence"—"happy" here means apt, fortunate and pleasing, rather than pleased, or (nearly vanished sense) happenstance. I like the way this third term in the sentence's brief inventory—the most concrete term, but not so very concrete—has been elongated, allowed to spread itself around. The absence of stricturing commas around "but anomalous" is in line with Didion's later style: she knows better than most when to leave out the commas for which other writers (or their editors) instinctively reach, to let grammar and a certain sonic ease do their work. The sentence sounds like Didion: in its rhythm, care and thrift, then also in the swerve towards something more troubling or mysterious, the suggestion in the final phrase of an impish curating personality at work in the house.

Was I right to think about the sentence in this way? Here is what I found when I turned from the *New York Times* to *Telling Stories* and Didion's more detailed account of her time at *Vogue*—an apprenticeship, she says, that is too easy to mock. At first she composed merchandising copy, and then promotional copy ("the distinction between the two was definite but recondite"), and eventually editorial copy, which included captions. "A sample of the latter," Didion writes:

Opposite, above: All through the house, colour, verve, improvised treasures in happy but anomalous coexistence. Here, a Frank Stella, an art nouveau stained-glass panel, a Roy Lichtenstein. Not shown: a table covered with frankly brilliant oilcloth, a Mexican find at fifteen cents a yard.

And the sentence, at least in this telling, is followed by another that opens out, shows us the incongruent treasures, includes again some nice economies—"a Mexican find," not "a find in Mexico"—and bright phrasing: the "frankly brilliant oilcloth."

But run it through again, because we're not quite there. On the desk in front of me—an eBay find at fifty dollars—I have the 1 August 1965 issue of American *Vogue*. In the way of popular magazines of that period, it reads now as a surprisingly highbrow artefact. There is a substantial feature on Giacometti, a movie review by Elizabeth Hardwick—*Ship of Fools*, from Katherine Anne Porter's novel—and (opposite) a report by Didion on the new National Museum of Anthropology in Mexico City: "one comes away remembering certain small things, haunted by oddities." Verbal novelty seems to exercise the editors of *Vogue* to an impressive degree. As the cover declares, the issue is devoted to the style, tastes and attitudes of a figure it calls "the young chicerino": an awkward coinage, obsolete precursor to "fashionista," that seems not to have existed much outside these pages. (*Vogue* had introduced the type exactly a year before: "Her presentation is perfect: she comes in a blaze of certainty, engages all interest, sustains it, provokes. Unhesitatingly she chooses what's good for her—the gesture, the look that conveys her mood, her quality, her special dash.") A few pages after Didion and Hardwick, the magazine announces its twenty-fifth Prix de Paris: "a career competition for college seniors," with the first prize of a year on the magazine as a Junior Editor, and a trip to Paris to see the shows. Didion herself had won the prize in 1956, with an essay on the California architect William Wilson Wurster. It was what brought her to New York; she turned down the Paris trip in favour of real work at the magazine. In 1965, competition entrants are asked to identify teenage fashion trends, suggest a person to cover for the "People Are Talking About" section and, in an exercise that sounds thoroughly Talmey-esque, to propose alternative words or phrases for "Bargains in Chic," "The Young Chicerino," "Accessories," "Shop Hound" and "Fashions in Living."

Didion's caption appears in the "Fashions in Living" department, alongside a culinary conversation with Paul Newman and Joanne Woodward, and a short drinks feature titled "Through Deepest Summer with Zest and Cube." The piece to which Didion contributed is called "The Loved House of the Dennis Hoppers"—the now dated plural denoting both Hopper and his actor wife Brooke Hayward—and was written by the novelist and screenwriter Terry Southern, with photographs of house and family by Hopper himself. Southern's tone is insiderish, hipster-New-Journalist, a touch embarrassing even for its time. His opening paragraph: "The Den Hoppers are tops in their field. Precisely what their field is, is by no means certain—except that she is a Great Beauty, and he is a kind of Mad Person." Southern essays a zany tour of Hopper's acting career, his politics (a "jaunt" to photograph the Selma marches earlier that year), counter-cultural affiliations (Ginsberg, *et al.*) and his art collection, on which subject Southern solicits an approving comment from Frank O'Hara. It's an entertaining, imprecise and exhausting sort of writing, rather like its author's description of his subject: "To walk down a city street with him is like being attached to a moving adrenaline pump."

There is energy of a kind in the captions too, but it is coolly and rigorously contained. "*Left*, Mrs. Hopper, who is the actress Brooke Hayward, poses in a red leather chair for Robert Walker junior. The pillow reads 'Long May It Wave.'" Or this: "To visit the Hopper house is to be, at every turn, surprised, freshly beguiled by a kaleidoscopically shifting assemblage of found objects, loved objects, *objets d'art*." And some of those objects: "*Opposite page, below*, on the dining room walls, a 1907 Budweiser girl and a Chéret poster. In the hall, one of several streetlights in the house. On the living room wall: a Marcel Duchamp found object; above it, the Mona Lisa in duplicate by Andy Warhol."

At the bottom of the first page of the piece, one finds the passage Didion quotes in *Telling Stories*—the passage then cited by the *New York Times* and, as "an early example" of her *Vogue* editorial copy, by Didion's biographer Tracy Daugherty. Or rather, you find this: "*Opposite, above*, through the house, colour, verve, things in happy, anomalous coexistence. Here, a Frank Stella painting, an art nouveau stained glass panel, a Roy Lichtenstein painting." What has happened, exactly? Let us stick with the first sentence for now. Never mind the italics, a convention of these captions which Didion might be expected to leave out later, when she quotes herself. Never mind the comma instead of a colon. Though I have always liked the habit—now mostly American—of a capital letter after a colon, as if a whole new sentence were starting up, and I would quite like to linger on what it does and what it means. Onwards, to the most obvious difference. It is of course this: "things in happy, anomalous coexistence." *Things*. In the caption as printed on page 138 of *Vogue*, the word comes three lines from the bottom, at the right-hand limit of a run of short nouns: "house, colour, verve, things." (I feel justified in treating the sentence in this line-by-line fashion, because Didion tells us that she was working within not only strict word limits, but character counts too: the shape of available space on the page mattered.) *Things*—it subtracts from the rhythm of the sentence heard aloud, and seems in all respects a feeble word choice, inexact and thin.

Except, except: recall that line of Didion's in her piece about the Mexican museum. Here is the whole sentence: "Inside, the collection is too overwhelming to see all at once; one comes away remembering certain small things, haunted by oddities." Sometimes, in the face of profusion, when tempted by treasures, you need instead a word as unshowy as "things," which is anyway given *a certain* (how she loves this phrasing!) Didion flavour, which rescues it from banality. The caption is seventeen lines long, printed in small sans-serif type, with (unlike the main feature) a ragged right-hand edge. And it starts like this: "Up in the Hollywood Hills, above the Sunset Strip, Mr. and Mrs. Dennis Hopper (portraits, above *left*) have a house of such gaiety and wit that it seems the result of some marvellous scavenger hunt, full of improvised treasures, the bizarre and the beautiful and the banal in wild juxtaposition, everything the *most* of its kind." There they are, the "improvised treasures," as if some careless admiring guest has picked them up and put them down again in the wrong place. It's not the only phrase in Didion's remembered version of her caption that looks like it's been moved from where we first found it. Here again is the second sentence, from 1965: "Here, a Frank Stella painting, an art nouveau stained glass panel, a Roy Lichtenstein painting." And the version she gives us in 1978: "Here, a Frank Stella, an art-nouveau stained-glass panel, a Roy Lichtenstein." So much better without the repeated "painting." And what about the thing not shown: "a table covered with frankly brilliant oilcloth, a Mexican find at fifteen cents a yard"? Actually, that is shown, but four pages further on, with caption: "Everywhere in the Hopper house the point is to amuse, to delight. *Near right, above*, in the breakfast room, the table covered with brilliant oilcloth, a Mexican find at fifteen cents a yard."

Enough detail, enough quotation. Between 1965 and 1978, what goes on? What is Didion doing and why should I, let alone you, care? When I first found these small disparities I was seized with the sort of excitement that must overtake real scholars when they discover, for example, telling variations among printed or manuscript copies of the same great poem. But a photo caption from a fashion magazine, a scrap of anonymous juvenilia from a writer who even then was publishing far more skilful and profound and savvy pieces? How could such a small detail matter? Except it did, or does, to Joan Didion, enough to pull these sentences from—where? From a handwritten or typed original? In which case perhaps the printed version is evidence of Talmey's editing and Didion's rewriting, with fragments of the first effort—"run it through again, sweetie"—dispersed about the magazine's pages? Or (and I vastly prefer this possibility) Didion has gone to the magazine—it would not be unusual to keep your early periodical appearances around for thirteen years, or longer—and improved upon the version she wrote in 1965.

Reviewing Didion's novel *Democracy* in 1984, Mary McCarthy wondered about the relationship between ethics and style in Didion's work—and not only there, but in literature, and life, in general. "Is the ear the ultimate moral judge?" An attention to sound—to getting the right sound—in her writing has been for Didion a lifelong occupation. In *The Year of Magical Thinking* she tells us: "As a writer, even as a child, long before what I wrote began to be published, I developed a sense that meaning itself was resident in the rhythms of words and sentences and paragraphs, a technique for withholding whatever it was I thought or believed behind an increasingly impenetrable polish." She learned to hold on to her words, running them through until they sounded right and therefore were right.

She hears things, but she sees stuff too.

> The arrangement of the words matters; and the arrangement you want can be found in the picture in your mind. The picture dictates the arrangement. The picture dictates whether this will be a sentence with or without clauses, a sentence that ends hard or a dying-fall sentence, long or short, active or passive.

This is from "Why I Write," a piece Didion wrote for the *New York Times* in 1976. "The picture dictates the arrangement." You have to wonder where a writer would learn such a lesson, or learn to express it in such terms, if not from writing about actual pictures. For myself, at the age Didion was when she composed these captions for *Vogue*, I had been used only to writing about books, writing about words, writing about writing. I learned to write about everything else—what we might call *life*—by training myself to write about photographs. "I saw things I imagined." It is an excellent education in hearing the affinities between words and things, between the structure of a scene and the shape of a sentence. The picture dictates the arrangement: this is what I hear Joan Didion discovering in the sentence, then reminding herself of thirteen years later. She was getting used to writing, she said, about the kind of people who had Stellas and Lichtensteins and bargains from Mexico—but she was also just getting used to putting one thing beside another.

A Tour of the Monuments

"Noon-day sun cinema-ized the site, turning the bridge and the river into an over-exposed *picture*."

—ROBERT SMITHSON

IT IS 1967, and the land artist Robert Smithson is describing, in the pages of *Artforum*, his recent excursion from New York to the New Jersey town of Passaic, and environs. Smithson does not tell us that he was born in Passaic and grew up in adjacent Rutherford and then nearby Clifton, nor does he mention that the family physician was William Carlos Williams. But a modernist literary attitude saturates "A Tour of the Monuments of Passaic, New Jersey," the essay from which this sentence derives. With its accompanying black-and-white Instamatic snapshots of Passaic's crumbling downtown, post-industrial outskirts and half-built highway, the essay is an ironic hymn to modern ruins, a slightly stoned, slightly sci-fi expression of Smithson's art of territorial displacement and chronological exile.

Smithson takes a bus from the Port Authority Building in Manhattan to the outskirts of Rutherford, then crosses a bridge over the Passaic River: it is on the bridge that he stops first to observe and describe the landscape, as if he were a genteel naturalist of the nineteenth century, or an intrepid traveller in search of the picturesque at the end of the eighteenth. On his bus ride, Smithson has been reading the *New York Times*—an article touching on Samuel Morse's ruins painting, *Allegorical Landscape*, of 1836—and a science-fiction novel by Brian Aldiss called *Earthworks*. Smithson is already preoccupied by ruins of the past, and visions of future catastrophe. On the banks of the Passaic River, incongruously, he finds both. The scene is dotted with "relics" or "monuments"—pipes and cranes and pumps, pyramids of rubble and pits of sand—that suggest a lost civilization. Passaic, Smithson quips, has supplanted Rome and become the new Eternal City. But this landscape of classical-industrial desolation also argues, as ruins always do, some disastrous future, "Utopia minus a bottom, a place where the machines are idle, and the sun has turned to glass."

Smithson's writing is filled with such post-apocalyptic imagery, some of it borrowed from, or indebted to, contemporaries such as J. G. Ballard. There are echoes too of *The Waste Land*, references to Borges and to Nabokov, who wrote in an early short story: "The future is but the obsolete in reverse." "A Tour of the Monuments" bristles with artefacts from Smithson's voracious, but likely unmethodical, reading. A novelist I know

recently told me that while he finds Smithson's art and writings
("A Tour of the Monuments" in particular) to be inspiring for
what it says about exurban America, and about artistic efforts
to capture territory in words or images, he finds himself quite
allergic to the style and texture of Smithson's prose—he longs,
in fact, to take an editor's pencil to the page. I think I can see
what he objects to. Here for instance is all of the paragraph
from which this sentence comes:

> The bus passed over the first monument. I pulled the buzzer-
> cord and got off at the corner of Union Avenue and River
> Drive. The monument was a bridge that connected Bergen
> County with Passaic County. Noon-day sunshine cinema-ized
> the site, turning the bridge and the river into an over-exposed
> *picture*. Photographing it with my Instamatic 400 was like
> photographing a photograph. The sun became a monstrous
> light-bulb that projected a detached series of "stills" through
> my Instamatic into my eye. When I walked on the bridge, it
> was as though I was walking on an enormous photograph that
> was made of wood and steel, and underneath the river existed
> as an enormous movie film that showed nothing but a contin-
> uous blank.

I like the awkward, both tortured and too casual, way that
Smithson insists on his main conceit in this passage. To look
at this landscape—unreal outskirts of an unreal city—is to see

yourself seeing. The place is already an image, so making images of it involves a plunge into tautology, repetition and recursiveness. Likewise Smithson's paragraph, which is not content with the initial image alone, but must force the point home. An *enormous* photograph, an *enormous* film. The sun is a lightbulb, the camera is an eye, the eye in its turn a screen, the river a screen too, on which is projected—nothing. (Smithson might have been thinking of the Korean artist Nam June Paik's 1964 film, *Zen for Film*, which consists of eight minutes of blank white leader: a cinematic homage to John Cage's silent composition *4″33′*.)

Why should this sentence, above all others, and more than Smithson's accompanying snapshots of his fanciful "monuments," persist in the mind? For sure, the sentence has its smoother, unifying qualities: the sibilance of "sunshine cinema-ized the site," the metric heft of that first clause, which is stretched and even squandered in the second half of the sentence. Perhaps the italics are necessary after all, in a clause that otherwise threatens to fade out weakly at its end? Isn't the whole thing also, in some ways—the clumsiness of "cinema-ized," the fact the sentence is more generally hyphen-happy, the needlessly emphasized *picture*—an inelegant "heap of language"? This phrase is the title of a text-cum-drawing Smithson completed in 1966, a triangular or mountain-shaped pile of pencilled words about words: "Language/phraseology speech/tongue lingo vernacular/mother tongue King's English/dialect

brogue patois idiom . . ." A verbless sentence of sorts. Maybe
this is the point: a sentence as container for the rubble of meaning, like one of the artist's sculpted "non-sites": portions of
unruly landscape or geology relocated to the white cube of the
gallery.

In the spring of 2006 I took a bus from the Port Authority
Building to the edge of Rutherford, where I got out and walked
to the river. The crosshatched iron and wood bridge on which
Smithson stood in 1967 had long gone, replaced by a dull concrete span. I was trying to follow Smithson's route along the
Passaic and into town, but the highway, which was under construction when he wrote "A Tour of the Monuments," had
finally been finished and now blocked my way. After studying
various maps back home, I had concluded there was a point
not far from the end of the bridge where it must be possible
to cross and soon turn off into suburban Passaic. I emailed the
City Manager and asked if it was safe. "On no account cross
the highway—you will die." But I had no choice. I set off under
a cloudless sky, looking for new ruins, trying to hear as well as
see the broken aesthetic Smithson brought (or brought back)
to the place. "Noon-day sunshine cinema-ized the site, turning
the bridge and the river into an over-exposed *picture*."

It Is Only a Paper Dagger

"Singular perspective the lady had as she looked about the room in which nothing was real except her blue eyes."

—MAEVE BRENNAN

THE SENTENCE ITSELF is all perspective, practically a dance of gazes. It is 1968, and the Irish writer Maeve Brennan—author of perfectly wrought fictions, precise and pitiless essayist under her *New Yorker* pen-name The Long-Winded Lady—is once more out in Manhattan, keenly attentive, at a distance, to the people she sees: their small urban dramas and likely epic interior narratives. Brennan has spotted this woman at the University Restaurant on West Eighth Street as she hurries in with a hand to her "silver-beige" hair, wearing a pale raincoat and a dark-grey linen dress.

She was svelte and good-looking, with very white skin, and blue eyes that glanced around the restaurant with a fixed, dispassionate expression as though it were habitual with her not to be interested. As some people give meaning to everything they touch, the lost lady seemed to look merely to exclude.

Brennan calls her "the lost lady" throughout her essay: the title was attached to the piece when it was first republished, in her 1969 collection *The Long-Winded Lady*. This other lady does not at first appear lost. She seems to know precisely where she is and how to comport herself there. Settling herself alone in a booth, she lights a cigarette, ignores the menu and refuses a drink: she is waiting for somebody. The inevitable husband, "a tall, narrow man, with sharp corners for shoulders," probably handsome when he was seventeen, turns up smiling and chatting, plucks the cigarette from between his wife's fingers and stubs it out. He orders her a whiskey, grabs the menu, and starts talking about his day. He only stops talking to examine a bottle of wine, while the lost lady sips her drink and purses her lips, and finally refuses her dinner: "I'm not really hungry anymore." She says it, Brennan writes, as if she were telling her faded, garrulous husband: "I am taking the shuttle to Boston," or "I am going to poison you tonight," or "It is time for a new frying pan."

Soon Brennan has to leave the restaurant, but not before she reaches this conclusion: "I think one of these people was a redeemer—or a saviour, if you prefer saviour—but whether the lost lady married her husband in the hope of saving him from something or other or married him in the hope that he would save her from something or other I do not know." (Note how any hope, of whatever variety, belongs to the wife, not the husband.) Isn't there something of this chiasmic puzzle in the sentence that appears at the end of Brennan's first paragraph? "Singular perspective the lady had as she looked about the room in which nothing was real except her blue eyes." The inversion in those first five words! Instead of saying: "The lady had a singular perspective…" At the outset, we're already in the shot-reverse-shot standoff between the gaze of the lost lady and the world that looks back at her: husband, writer, restaurant diners and decor, and of course Brennan herself, unseen protagonist of the essay, who sees all, and sees her subject seeing. The sentence makes me think of John Donne, in "The Good-Morrow": "My face in thine eye, thine in mine appears." Or in "The Extasie": "Our eye-beams twisted, and did thread/ Our eyes upon one double string." Except: the lost lady has no love, seems past all that, for anything she sees. "Customers sitting in booths, old-fashioned costume paintings, dark and romantic on the walls, salt and pepper shakers and lighted candles on all the tables"—the whole scene looks to her as if it's just an elaborate wallpaper design.

Look again at the sentence. "Singular perspective the lady had as she looked about the room in which nothing was real except her blue eyes." Perhaps I've not been quite accurate about the back-and-forth of gazes; it reads now like a panoramic photograph taken inside a hall of mirrors. We see as the lost lady sees, or rather does not see because none of it is real to her, and before we know it (no punctuation to make us pause for breath) we are part of the dream or diorama too, we've been merged with the unreal city, become a figment of those blue eyes. When you travel, Elizabeth Hardwick once wrote, the first lesson you learn is that you do not exist. It's a fearful lesson to have to learn at home, or rather in the city you are still hoping is home, as the Long-Winded Lady hopes. In the decades after she wrote these words, Brennan's own mental tether to the world frayed and then broke, weakened by drink and divorce. She wrote in one of her essays that there were now too many homes to feel homesick about. For a time, she was homeless, and is said to have slept in the bathrooms at *The New Yorker*. In "The Lost Lady," and in this miniature maze of a sentence, it is possible to see as she does her coming detachment from it all.

To Eat Is Not to Respect a Menu

"The eel (or the piece of vegetable, of shellfish), crystallized in grease, like the Branch of Salzburg, is reduced to a tiny clump of emptiness, a collection of perforations: here the foodstuff joins the dream of a paradox: that of a purely interstitial object, all the more provocative in that this emptiness is produced in order to provide nourishment (occasionally the foodstuff is constructed in a ball, like a wad of air)."

—ROLAND BARTHES

ROLAND BARTHES IS THE PATRON SAINT of my sentences, the writer whose habits while inside the sentence, as well as ideas about the sentence, are always on my mind. Without his prose pyrotechnics—"the Northern Lights in summer," said Elizabeth Hardwick—I would never have written a word. Absent the calm, titled fragments by which he structured his books and essays, I would not have found the courage to start amassing sentences and paragraphs of my own, never mind articles and essays, let alone books. His tone: analytic but entranced. His style: epigrammatic, ruefully aware that epigrams are fragile rhetorical artefacts, and you need to distract with another as soon as you can. In the name of—what? A truth made of accumulated sidelong glances, and not the frontal assault of critique or the dogged undermining of theory. Which is how a critic—is that really the word for Barthes?—becomes the most *seductive* writer I know.

The sentence appears in Barthes's 1970 book, *Empire of Signs*, which he wrote following three month-long visits to Japan in the late 1960s. Earlier in 1970, Barthes published *S/Z*, his fragmented study of a novella by Balzac called *Sarrasine*. Barthes divided the story into 561 fragments, which he glossed in turn according to five codes: hermeneutic, semic, symbolic, proairetic and cultural. *Sarrasine* is the eponymous tale of an apprentice sculptor who falls in love with Zambinella, a star of the Roman opera (described here in Clara Bell's translation):

> La Zambinella displayed in her single person, intensely alive and delicate beyond words, all those exquisite proportions of the female form which he had so ardently longed to behold, and of which a sculptor is the most severe and at the same time the most passionate judge. She had an expressive mouth, eyes instinct with love, flesh of dazzling whiteness.

Zambinella is in fact a man, a *castrato* who plays along with Sarrasine's misapprehension but refuses to be seduced by him.

When the truth is revealed, Sarrasine declares he will kill Zambinella, but instead he is stabbed to death on the orders of the singer's patron.

S/Z and *Empire of Signs* form a sort of hinge or gutter between Barthes's strictly academic work—schooled on and extending the methods of structuralism and semiotics—and the more personal, more "writerly" books he completed later in the decade: *Roland Barthes par Roland Barthes*, *A Lover's Discourse* and *Camera Lucida*. Already, in *Empire of Signs*, a subjective voice takes over from the theorist and cultural critic; Barthes seems more present on the page, body and soul, vulnerable but not exactly needy. At times in this book, as he describes his impressions of Japanese theatre, architecture, pop culture and aesthetic temperament, he is still the semiotician, naming the codes by which a society constitutes itself. Just as frequently, he is a writer seduced by the texture of things, casting certain captivating details in the most *particular* language he can find.

Empire of Signs is also, notoriously, a book that shamelessly declares, even celebrates, its author's distance from his subject: Barthes is not quite a tourist, but he does not know the language, and falls easily into clichés about Japan (and worse, "the orient") as a set of exotic surfaces. Barthes knows perfectly well that he has rendered Japan and the Japanese as culpably *other*. Still, he is fascinated, and when it comes to accusations of Eurocentrism there is, perhaps, a kind of amnesty if not exemption in his commitment to describing that fascination, which is not very different from the grazing (his word) mode of attention Barthes brings to most subjects.

The section containing the sentence comes around twenty pages into *Empire of Signs*; it is the last of four reflections on Japanese habits of cooking and eating. It is probably no surprise to find the delicately anatomizing critic who wrote *S/Z* also treating Japanese cuisine as if it were a type of writing, a species of text, even a utopian image of artistic or literary composition —not consumption. The disposition of food on table or tray is first of all, says Barthes, a kind of painting, then a sort of game, like chess. But in Barthes's laconic analysis the art or contest in question quickly turns into a manner of inscription:

> Japanese food establishes itself within a reduced system of substance (from the clear to the divisible), in a shimmer of the signifier: these are the elementary characters of the writing, established upon a kind of vacillation of language, and indeed this is what Japanese food appears to be: a written food, tributary to the gestures of division and selection.

A pair of chopsticks is like an inked brush or pen: it points, discerns, invents and describes, and all within an uncentred array that resembles nothing so much as Barthes's way of composing his own work: "on the table, on the tray, food is never anything but a collection of fragments."

So is the sentence, after its fashion. Barthes's translator, the American poet Richard Howard, has preserved the sparse but strangely excessive punctuation in the original. Here is the sentence in French:

L'anguille (ou le fragment de légume, de crustacé), cristallisée dans la friture, comme le rameau de Salzbourg, se réduit à un petit bloc de vide, à une collection de jours : l'aliment rejoint ici le rêve d'un paradoxe : celui d'un objet purement interstitiel, d'autant plus provoquant que ce vide est fabriqué pour qu'on s'en nourrisse (parfois l'aliment est construit en boule, comme une pelote d'air).

Two colons, *two* sets of parentheses? These are freedoms most writers, in English at any rate, might allow themselves in a first draft, but would likely subtract or replace (or have changed for them by an editor) in some later iteration. Barthes does both things all the time—his sentences are frequently perforated by parentheses as if nothing may pass before his gaze without some nuance or qualification attached. For a long time, in essays at school and university, and in the first things I wrote for publication, I hoped to emulate his use of colons: they seem to function so frequently like semicolons or dashes: they make something happen: rather than issuing onto, introducing an example or list, they mark a transformation: inside the sentence, outside in the world.

But the aspect of this sentence that I most admire—it might be the quirk of thought and word I love best in Barthes—is not really happening in its structure, syntax or punctuation. It is instead a movement or motif that's everywhere in his writing but hardly ever spoken about. It has to do not with signs or signification, but states of matter. Barthes is forever describing a moment when one substance becomes, or is revealed to be, another, adjacent or antithetical. It's his take on metaphor, his version of the poetic, a transubstantiating miracle he discovers time and again in the writers and artists (including the artists of Japanese cuisine) he regards with wonder and delight.

In Barthes's early book about Jules Michelet, the nineteenth-century French historian's life and work are cast repeatedly in terms of organic processes. Michelet has a menstrual obsession; he pictures the French people as a sanguinary resource, bubbling up through history; he thinks of the past as a field that he grazes, like an animal. There is a lot of food in Barthes's writings. In *Mythologies*, the meaning of steak and chips: the bloodiness of the meat connoting an idea of France, or land and produce and people. The passage in his almost-autobiography, *Roland Barthes par Roland Barthes*, where he lists his likes and dislikes. (Right now, all I remember is that he likes pears, being by then a little pear-shaped himself.) Sometimes foodstuffs arrive unexpectedly in his work. He reminds us that Sade disapproved of bread, "a pestilential amalgamation of flour and water," which had the un-Sadean effect of unfitting the subject for acts of coprophagia. In the same book (*Sade/Fourier/Loyola*), Barthes introduces the utopian thought of Charles Fourier with a curious anecdote about his own misadventures with Moroccan *smen*: "One day, I was invited to eat a couscous with rancid butter; the rancid butter was customary; in certain regions it is an integral part of the couscous code. However, be it prejudice, or unfamiliarity, or digestive intolerance, I don't like rancidity." Fourier would have helped, he says: he would say that Barthes's reaction was not idle or frivolous, "and that debating it is no more futile than debating transubstantiation."

In *Empire of Signs* substances constantly surprise—a foodstuff can easily turn into its opposite, or rather what a Western gaze or sensibility imagines to be the opposite. In "tempura," for example, the "sheath" of batter ("a golden milk") around a piece of shrimp or pepper is so delicate it resembles lace. And the oil in which it is fried is not the dense, turgid liquid we are used to:

> The oil (but is this oil—are we really dealing with the maternal substance, *the oily*?), immediately soaked up by the paper napkin on which you are served your *tempura* in a little wicker basket—the oil is dry, utterly unrelated to the lubricant with which the Mediterranean and the Near East cover their cooking and their pastry; it loses a contradiction which marks our foodstuffs cooked in oil or grease, which is to burn without

heating; this cold burning of the fat body is here replaced by a quality which seems denied to all fried food: freshness.

Who is to say whether Barthes is right about this or other culinary particularities? What would *right* mean, when it comes to the expression of such partial impressions? I think what excites him is not the possibility that he has exposed, in this small observation about Japanese cooking, a larger or deeper truth about Japan. What thrills Barthes, whether he is in a restaurant in Tokyo or Paris, whether he is paying attention to his own desires and tastes or, in the sentences of some writer he loves, to the subtle, voracious movement of another's desire, what quickens his heart is the spectacle, maybe only the fantasy, of this kind of transformation. His method, or better his style, is not to say: see how I have revealed this fraudulent world to be other than it pretends. But instead: look, watch with me, while this part of the world, at the pressure of fantasy, desire or interpretation, *becomes.* (Which is perhaps also the force of Balzac's "Sarrasine"; the "truth" of Zambinella's sex is only part of the point: even after she has confessed she occupies an androgynous place that Sarrasine, in his rage, cannot even name.)

And so, the sentence. How many sorts of transformation are at work in it? There is first of all a minor vacillation: the eel may also be a vegetable, or a shellfish. Second, this fragment is "crystallized" in grease: a strange description, for sure, conjuring already a purity and delicacy at odds with the actions

147

of battering and frying. And the Branch of Salzburg? The reference arrives by way of Stendhal's 1822 book *On Love*, where the novelist identifies seven stages of passion, from admiration to a final "crystallization" in which all elements of the loved being, even (or especially) the person's faults, are subsumed into the lover's favourable view of him or her. An anecdote explains the metaphor of the crystal:

> At the salt mines of Salzburg a branch stripped of its leaves by winter is thrown into the abandoned depths of the mine; taken out two or three months later it is covered with brilliant crystals; the smallest twigs, those no stouter than the leg of a sparrow, are arrayed with an infinity of sparkling, dazzling diamonds; it is impossible to recognise the original branch.

In Barthes's appropriation of Stendhal's image, there is a venerable cliché at work: cooking as an act of love or care, towards foodstuffs as much as the family or friends to whom they are offered. But something else too: a sense that with the proper loving attention a morsel of Japanese food will reveal itself to be fantastically metaphorical, just as a piece of language— poem, story, autobiographical fragment—will also do under the critic's touch.

"A collection of perforations...a purely interstitial object...a wad of air." We are hardly a third of the way through it when the sentence starts to empty itself out, becoming

148

lighter and less dense, aerated. So light in fact that I had forgotten for a moment the earlier "tiny clump of emptiness." So
many variations on the assertion that something is scarcely
there. In some ways, we are already in the territory of what
Barthes would later call "the neutral": that mode or mood in
which it is possible to refuse the heaviness of binary distinctions, to delay the moment when the wavering scale decides.
How to stay in this moment or this interstice, which is for
Barthes a way of talking about what he most values in art and
politics and intimate life? One way was to make sentences like
this one, in which the punctuation—those implacable colons
—keeps opening onto yet more subtly distinct possibilities, in
which "clump," "collection," "object," "ball" and "wad" are more
or less interchangeable, more or less neutral names for the same
thing. An act of blithe refusal or shyness—like the ambiguous
Zambinella turning down the advances of Sarrasine. A provocative reserve: what would that sound like, or read like, in a
sentence? Eventually, Barthes's sentence parcels itself up, "a
wad of air," in enclosing parentheses, like a balloon attached
to the end of the sentence (and the end of this essay), which
has now grown light enough for me to let it go.

Albeit Succoured by a Cult

"Parker's medium-tempo blues had a glittering, monolithic quality, and his fast blues were multiplications of his slow blues."

—WHITNEY BALLIETT

HAVING NO DEVELOPED KNOWLEDGE of jazz or its commentators, I have only just heard of Whitney Balliett, who was a jazz critic for *The New Yorker* from the mid-1950s until 2001. Look him up: there he is in his horn-rims, every inch the studious WASP enthusiast for the hottest nights and hippest cuts. *Whitney Balliett*, what a name. I have read that he frequently wore a bow tie.

There are several anthologies of Balliett's jazz writings: the first published in 1960 and the last in 2006, a year before his death. I intend to buy one of them soon; I've a special weakness for these magazine writers, critics especially, whose heyday was too early for me to have known, and who have never attained the renown or glamour of a Joseph Mitchell or Maeve Brennan, a Pauline Kael or Kenneth Tynan. (The *echt* exemplar: novelist and critic Penelope Gilliatt, who was understudy to both Tynan and Kael.) Soberly suited sidemen, backing singers in gowns more classically cut than the star's, Balliett seems like one of these: his brilliance surfaces fleetingly out of *The New Yorker*'s online archive, catching my ear and eye. Wait, *this* has been there all along?

The sentence is in "Bird," a piece about some reissues of Charlie Parker, published in March 1976. This article is so far the only thing I have read by Whitney Balliett. It seems that his longer profiles—he learned this skill from the likes of Mitchell—are masterpieces of extended quotation, the writer disappearing for pages at a time behind the voice of his subject, or his subject's intimates. There is some of this in the Parker piece, even twenty-one years after the saxophonist's death; out of Ross Russell's 1973 biography *Bird Lives!* the anecdotes of friends, and even Parker's doctor, supply an oral-history aspect. But the piece is mostly Balliett, elegantly corralling the chaos of Parker's short life, and reminding us why we should care— that is, telling us what Parker sounded like.

George Bernard Shaw once set out to write regular concert reviews without using any adjectives. Idiot. On the evidence of this one piece, Whitney Balliett's prose is an excellent argument for a descriptive and critical writing that is exuberantly adjectival. From this piece alone: "labyrinthine," "baffling," "askew," "husky," "loafing," "hymnlike," "chattering," "muscled," "glittering," "monolithic." But Balliett knows when not to overdo the adjectives, and overdo the verbs instead. On Parker's playing: "He cajoled, he attacked, he mourned, he sang, he laughed, he cursed." Or here is Balliett on Parker's solos:

> He would begin a solo with a purposely stuttering four- or five-note announcement, pause for effect, repeat the phrase, bending its last note into silence, turn the phrase around backward and abruptly slip into double time, zigzag up the scale, circle around at the top, and plummet, the notes falling somewhere between silence and sound. (Parker was a master of dynamics and of the dramatic use of silence.) Another pause, and he would begin his second chorus with a dreaming, three-note figure, each of the notes running into the next and each held in prolonged, hymnlike fashion. He would shatter this brief spell by inserting two or three short arpeggios, disconnected and broken off, then he would float into a loafing half time and shoot into another climbing-and-falling double-time run, in which he would dart in and out of nearby keys. He would pause, then close the chorus with an amen figure resembling his opening announcement.

Now, I love this passage too: among other things, it's a beautifully articulated comment on the cliché that one could write in such a way as to replicate the rhythms and textures of jazz. Balliett's prose does not honk, it does not stutter, it risks no unruly runs or riffs (though he is not immune to alliteration or assonance). Instead, all is in the structure, a topic with which Balliett is much exercised in this essay. Parker's approach to playing standards, he tells us, was to take apart the structure of the piece and replace it with a much more complex structure, with here and there hints of the original composition showing through.

Let's run through the sentence again. "Parker's medium-tempo blues had a glittering, monolithic quality, and his fast blues were multiplications of his slow blues." The sentence comes directly after the long passage I quoted above, with its succession of "woulds"—Parker would do this, and he would do that—and the shift to the plain past tense signals a clarifying or consolidating sentence. Or better: "crystallizing." Everything is suddenly static; the overactive verbs fall away, leaving only "had" and "were." Hard to say, though, that the sentence itself has a "glittering, monolithic quality": for all his craft, Balliett is far too modest for prose monuments. Observe the economies of the sentence: the solid paired adjectives, for a start. How strange, you might say, after the convoluting movements of the previous sentence, to claim that Parker's music has something solid and immobile about it. But doesn't "glittering, monolithic" also sound like it describes a mirage? Some things are fixed and certain in this sentence: the repetition of "blues," for sure, except that the plain word is involved, just like the music, in complex, prismatic, crystalline variations.

What does "multiplication" mean, exactly, in this context? At first I imagined a frenzied accumulation of already existing forms—but that doesn't do justice to what Balliett is describing here. Instead: an intensification, complexification, the glittering monolith now giving off sparks.

How to describe such intricate experiences, even vexingly opaque or discombobulating experiences, in language that will take your reader there but allow her to remain sufficiently calm and distant that it all makes sense? In his minor art of jazz criticism, or jazz description, Whitney Balliett invents the most compact and recursive structure, which holds up phrases of extreme daring. The sentence remains mysterious, which is perhaps why, when I first copied it out to serve as the heading for this fragment, I must have tried unconsciously to multiply, somehow thus to explain, its effects: "Parker's medium-tempo blues had a glittering, monolithic quality, and his fast blues were multiplications of his slow blues *were multiplications of his slow blues*."

The Cunning of Destruction

"In her presence on these tranquil nights it was possible to experience the depths of her disbelief, to feel sometimes the mean, horrible freedom of a thorough suspicion of destiny."

—ELIZABETH HARDWICK

"TO WAKE UP IN THE MORNING under a command to animate the stones of an idea, the clods of research, the uncertainty of memory, is the punishment of the vocation." This is how Elizabeth Hardwick once described the rigours of being an essayist. She took her punishment in style. As a writer of fiction, she had a couple of early misfires with her novels *The Ghostly Lover* (1945) and *The Simple Truth* (1955), followed by the obliquely fragmented triumph of the svelte, semi-autobiographical fiction *Sleepless Nights* (1979). She spent most of her writing life at or near the heart of a liberal American literary establishment. Her marriage to the poet Robert Lowell, whom she eventually divorced, obscured her

achievements for a time. She was part of a group that estab-
lished the *New York Review of Books* in 1963; the magazine's
founding editors Robert Silvers and Barbara Epstein had been
partly inspired by a mordant *Harper's* article of Hardwick's on
the decline of book reviewing. In common with the work of
many great essayists, her best pieces start out as book reviews
and far exceed the form—best because most acute, most peculiar, most daring in pursuit of an elegantly weird style.

The sentence in question appears midway through a piece
about Billie Holiday that Hardwick published in the *NYRB*
of 4 March 1976. (There is a version of the sentence, much
inferior, in *Sleepless Nights*, but let's leave that alone for now.)
In her mid-twenties, she had befriended the singer in New
York. In darkling fashion, her essay recalls textures and spectacles of the 1940s: the "underbrush" of cheap hotel interiors,
fingertips split while rummaging through second-hand record
racks, the bird-like figures of great jazz musicians as they
stooped out of taxis and into the clubs. And at the centre of it
all, the "puzzling phantom" of Holiday herself, who is heard
to speak only once in the whole piece. Her character leaches
out instead in performance, in relations with her tired and
flummoxed entourage, in vignettes of addiction, illness, impris-
onment. Most of all in the odd, skewed language Hardwick
has fashioned to evoke her, with its vexing repetitions and sly
inversions: "She was fat the first time we saw her, large, brilliantly beautiful, fat."

How exactly to describe Hardwick's singular style? For sure, it is a kind of lyricism, a method that allows her as a critic to bring the reader close to her subject via the seductions first of sound and second of image and metaphor. (In the *Times Literary Supplement* in 1983, the British novelist David Lodge called Hardwick the first properly lyric critic since Virginia Woolf, but this cannot be true: the lyric mode is indispensable even to a criticism that imagines it's doing something quite else.) Joan Didion has approved Hardwick's "exquisite diffidence," and in an interview for the *Paris Review*, she herself remarked: "The poet's voice is one of my passions. I like the offhand flashes, the absence of the lumber in the usual prose." There is a sense always that Hardwick's sentences stand alone, pay little or no attention to one another, that each is a self-involved and sufficient whole. She advances (if that's the word) paratactically: impression piled upon impression, analogy stacked against analogy, till she runs out of conceits and gives it to us relatively strict and straight.

The metaphors in Hardwick's essays are always unusual, which is what one wants from a metaphor. They are often simply bizarre, or strained as far as they will go. She can be straightforwardly graceful and apposite, as in the opening sentence of "Bloomsbury and Virginia Woolf": "Bloomsbury is, just now, like one of those ponds on a private estate from which all of the trout have been scooped out for the season." But what are we to make of the moment when, having told us that Zelda

Fitzgerald's biography had been buried, she goes further and says that Zelda lies beneath the "desperate violets" of F. Scott Fitzgerald's memories? Hardwick, who had abandoned a dissertation on metaphysical poetry to become a writer, was ever committed to the vivid, cumbrous oddity that could be canvassed in metaphor.

Consider the possibilities broached in "Billie Holiday." Here is Hardwick describing a young trumpet player (most probably Joe Guy) with whom the singer had recently become involved: "He was as thin as a stick and his lovely, round, light face, with frightened, shiny, round eyes, looked like a sacrifice impaled upon the stalk of his neck." Or recalling Holiday's coiffure: "And always the lascivious gardenia, worn like a large, white, beautiful ear... Sometimes she dyed her hair red and the curls lay flat against her skull, like dried blood." Holiday's huge dogs, always present, are "like sculpted treasures, fit for the tomb of a queen." As an admirer and hanger-on of the perennially "over-scheduled" performer, "one felt like an old carriage horse standing at the entrance, ready for the cold midnight race through the park." In her most dismally concise image, Hardwick writes of Holiday's death: "The police were at the hospital bedside, vigilant lest she, in a coma, manage a last chemical inner migration."

And then there is this sentence—here it is again: "In her presence on these tranquil nights it was possible to experience the depths of her disbelief, to feel sometimes the mean, horrible freedom of a thorough suspicion of destiny." It is one of those Hardwickian moments when the figural falls away and we're faced, she and we, with the calamitous, gnomic essence of her subject: a woman who has never been a Christian, who cannot believe in family—Holiday's mother fusses at the edges of the essay—and still less in the men she meets. A person whose sole commitments are to her "felonious narcotism" and perhaps to her art. The realization is stark, and unadorned by simile. But it is also not simple: it was "possible," merely, to apprehend (or is it to inhabit?) Holiday's absence of faith, and then only "sometimes." Why?

Of course it is a beautiful sentence, perfectly weighted, its comma-pivoting parallelism drawing on venerable lessons about the rhetorical virtues of repetition with difference. Some writers, or editors, might have thrown the delicate thing off by inserting a comma after "nights." (Hardwick's commas are always well placed. She was a connoisseur of twinned adjectives with comma, as in "mean, horrible.") As the sentence stands, that first comma is something like the hinge of the whole essay. Either side of it sits a pleasingly sinister decor of alliteration— all those plosives in the first part of the sentence, and sibilants in the second—as well as the slow, maybe drawled, but definitive diagnosis of "a thorough suspicion of destiny." (Which phrase, by the way, is remarkably unclear in its meaning.)

Hardwick's syntax is seamless here, and seductive, but the sentence is rattled by the ghost of an ambiguity that is general

159

in her writing. The best example I can think of is the opening sentence of her 1956 *Partisan Review* essay "America and Dylan Thomas": "He died, grotesquely like Valentino, with mysterious, weeping women at his bedside." Was the poet's death grotesque? No doubt, but, shifting the first comma back a word, Hardwick tells us as much and something more—the grotesquerie was not even his own, which in itself is grotesque. Subclauses are frequently strange and estranging in Hardwick; as Wayne Koestenbaum puts it in a short essay on his love for her sentences, an interjection or aside may arrive "like a great raw piece of beef soliciting our appetite."

Our sentence has its own exciting morsels. So much in Hardwick's prose depends upon her curious word choices. Often she favours the adjectival "-ing," as in the opening line of her *NYRB* obituary of Susan Sontag in 2005: "Except in unusually desolating circumstances, human beings do not want to die." "Desolating" does something that "desolate" would not: it points to a fragile passivity in the mortally minded person, and indicates a process that may or may not be coming to an end soon. In "Billie Holiday," there is "the freezing perception" that the star is feared by her own retinue. Note also Hardwick's use of the definite article—whose perception? And again in our sentence (our lesson?) "the mean, horrible freedom." We might say this sentence is all about—because it so economically undermines—the possibility of sympathy or proper identification. What of "mean" and "horrible"? They might as easily describe a willed state as a corralling predicament.

Here at last is the version of the sentence in *Sleepless Nights*:

> In her presence on these bedraggled nights, nights when performers all over the world were smiling, dancing, or pretending to be a prince of antiquity, offering their acts to dead rooms, then it was impossible to escape the depths of her disbelief, to refuse the mean, horrible freedom of a savage suspicion of destiny.

The adjectives are weaker because melodramatic—"bedraggled," "savage"—and the digressive global panorama of performers almost ruinously sentimental. But the main lapse from the version of 1976 is this: "the mean, horrible freedom" now cannot be fled or refused, so we're told, when in fact (in both versions) a failure or unwillingness to follow Holiday into her dauntless nihilism is all of the point. In the essay and the novel, the next sentence says: "And yet the heart always drew back from the power of her will and its engagement with disaster."

We do an injustice to Billie Holiday, writes Hardwick, if we imagine the value of her art to lie in the lyrics of the songs she sang. "Her message was otherwise. It was *style*." Which is to say—what? That she was ultimately in control of her art, or quite the opposite? For what is style if not precisely the oscillation, a refusal to choose, between mastery and accident, between determined artifice and ineludible character? Hard-wick liked to say that all her first drafts read as if they'd been written by a chicken. There was a deal of labour involved in becoming otherwise, in seeming or sounding not-chicken enough, and the sentence dramatizes that effort, for it was also a work of affinity and solicitude.

Suite Vénitienne

"I took a trip to see the beautiful things."

—Susan Sontag

THE SENTENCE IS SONTAG'S, but so much about it—the comic euphemism or at least evasion, the ironic tone, the deadpan dialogue of which it is part—belongs to Donald Barthelme, who she was trying to imitate and even surpass. It is the first sentence of Sontag's best (and maybe her only great) short story, "Unguided Tour," the final story in her 1978 collection *I, etcetera*. All of Sontag's fiction, good, bad and indifferent, is touchingly marked by striving: first, to be an experimentalist in the mode of the *nouveau roman*, finally to be a realist novelist on the grand scale and design of the nineteenth century. And in between, in the 1970s, to become a postmodernist (Sontag did not embrace the term) after the style of Barthelme, whose profound, hilarious, playful stories were then wildly fashionable. Barthelme seemed to have bundled the eminences of post-war fiction, and their particular skills—the merciless sentences of Beckett and Nabokov; the self-dismantling fictions of Borges and Robbe-Grillet; as well as the flaying of American surfaces in Pynchon, Updike and Roth—into a funhouse hall of mirrors. Still, his stories sounded like nobody else. Sontag's failed attempt to compose one of her own stands here for all the sentences in Barthelme's work I might have written about, including his one-sentence, seven-page, story titled "Sentence."

The resemblance, which I will let go of shortly, because it does not explain or exhaust "Unguided Tour," is all in the stilted vulnerability of the back-and-forth dialogue. Compare the opening lines of Barthelme's "The Apology" with "Unguided Tour":

—Sitting on the floor by the window with only part of my face in the window. He'll never come back.

—Of course he will. He'll return, open the gate with one hand, look up and see your face in the window.

—He'll never come back. Not now.

—He'll come back. New lines on his meagre face. Yet with head held high.

—I was unforgivable.

—I would not argue otherwise.

And Sontag:

I took a trip to see the beautiful things. Change of scenery.
    Change of heart. And do you know?
What?
They're still there.
Ah, but they won't be for long.
I know. That's why I went. To say goodbye.
Whenever I travel, it's always to say goodbye.

When she had done with "Unguided Tour," Sontag noted in
her diary that she had "written a better story than Barthelme."
We need not believe her, nor even forgive her this hubris, to
admit the strange brilliance of the piece. It's a story about
travel, memory, melancholy and the resistance to melancholy,
the consolations of art and culture, the skewing self-regard of
Americans in Europe, Westerners in general going everywhere
else, with their blindness to contemporary conditions and
politics in the places they visit, their fixations on relics of the
past. It is also about the disintegration of a relationship: "We
quarrelled most of the time. He plodding, I odious." There is
a lot here of Sontag herself, her ambitions and embarrassments.
She had carried on some of her most vexing love affairs in
Europe. Until late in life she was famously immune, like the
returned traveller in this story, to the attractions of nature: a
blind spot deriving, so the second voice in "Unguided Tour"
has it, from "too much indulgence in the nervous, metallic

pleasures of cities." Lovers and friends of Sontag's sometimes complained that she "had no eye" for the art and architecture she saw on her travels, no matter how committed she was to the idea of culture and the ideas by which you might understand it or talk about it. One might find oneself, for example, in front of a magnificent fresco or sculpture in Florence, being lectured at by Sontag instead of allowed to look.

What has this character, Sontag's stand-in, said goodbye to, exactly? The story is full of touristic clichés. There are the things themselves: "Tile roofs, timbered balconies, fish in the bay, the copper clock, shawls drying on the rocks, the delicate odour of olives, sunsets behind the bridge, ochre stone." And the conventional words and phrases uttered as one moves among those things (the italics are Sontag's): "*In the café...I'm sure...This spot...Nice...It says...Let's...*" Also, those moments when the tourist thinks to have stepped from her carapace of privilege and seen things as they really are—but of course the moment is already past: "Covered with flies. That poor child. Did you see?" All of this is a backdrop to a harsher set of judgements and self-judgements:

I don't want to satisfy my desire, I want to exasperate it. I want to resist the temptation of melancholy, my dear. If you only knew how much.

Then you must stop this flirtation with the past invented by poets and curators. We can forget about their old things.

166

We can buy their postcards, eat their food, admire their sexual nonchalance. We can march in their workers' festivals and sing the "Internationale," for even we know the words.

It's a short story after the style of Barthelme, for sure, but at moments like this, as in much of her fiction, Sontag cannot help sounding like her essayistic self: sententious, aphoristic, assured. Or like the self-lacerating voice of her diaries, trying always to disabuse herself of various types of sentiment, or despairing at the consequences of her lack of same. "Unguided Tour" gives us mostly the first, more brittle Sontag, and so it denies some of the pleasures, the ambiguities and weaknesses, we might look for in fiction. The other aspect of Barthelme's writing that Sontag's lacks: any trace of humour.

But something happened to transform this brilliant but hampered story: in 1983, Sontag directed a film based on it for Italian television. *Unguided Tour*, also known as *Letter from Venice*, makes the precise European location clear, and is as much a story about the city itself as about cities and travel in general, or about the couple who are its languorous protagonists. They are played by the Italian actor Claudio Cassinelli and the American dancer and choreographer Lucinda Childs, with whom Sontag was then in a relationship. Venice, says the film's opening narration, is "A tourist city different from any other. Different from Florence. Different from Siena. Different from Rome. Different from Athens. Or Dubrovnik." Because there's an imaginary kingdom of which this city is the capital. Venice is the capital of melancholy, in the way that Paris (according to Walter Benjamin) was the capital of the nineteenth century. The man and woman, without any clear plot to contain them, wander this glorious doleful city together, and she alone, narrating her impressions of Venice alongside the dissolution of their romance. There are tourists, gondolas and sumptuous interiors, a house with a hundred twirling wind toys on its facade, close-ups of decaying statuary, views of the gleaming lagoon, a flight of pigeons from behind Childs's head as she bickers with her lover at a café. And periodically, the stately presence of the dancer simply moving slowly and silently about the city. A lot of *Unguided Tour* reminds me of *Suite Vénitienne*, the artist Sophie Calle's clandestine photographic pursuit in Venice of a man she had met briefly at a party in Paris—the images and accompanying text were published in 1979.

And the sentence? What has happened to the sentence? It arrives around fourteen minutes into the seventy-minute film, with a shot of Childs, dressed in a yellow and black blouse, black skirt and boots, walking away from the camera in the sunshine, towards a small florist's shop, hardly more than a stall, beside an ornate gate. There are flower pots full of blooms on the pavement, a table with blue watering can, and the little store is faced with three large sheets of mirror, reflecting a handful of figures moving in or standing about the street. As

I write this I'm watching the scene on YouTube set to play at half speed so I don't miss a thing. (Is that what I've been trying to do with all of these sentences? To read them in slow motion? Would *reading in slow motion* mean you were more alert, or more stupid?) The soundtrack is in Italian, which I do not speak, and there are no English subtitles, but I have found the time-coded text of some subtitles elsewhere, and so I'm reading, alongside the film, a translation of the Italian script back into an English which is no longer Sontag's:

00:14:18,022 → 00:14:21,083
I went on a journey to see beautiful things.

Most of the irony has vanished along with the definite article. On screen, Lucinda Childs is approaching the flower stall—her black boots, almost to the knee, remind me of my mother's. In fuzzy video the silk of Childs's skirts sways and shines. And then a certain affinity strikes me: the elegant woman seen from behind as she enters the florist's, her image doubled in plate glass—the sequence recalls (is based on?) the famous moment in Alfred Hitchcock's *Vertigo* when Scottie (James Stewart) is secretly watching Madeleine (Kim Novak) as she buys the small bouquet of flowers that will complete her resemblance to a long-dead woman in a portrait, and set in motion a fatal mechanism of desire, longing and regret. *Unguided Tour* contains no such dramatic turns of plot or surprises of character.

169

But in locating her story in a real place with actual bodies, letting it unfold in mysterious composure, Sontag has turned her fussy attempt at a story to rival Barthelme, whose lightness she could never match, into a melancholic masterpiece. And this sentence is the point on which the whole thing turns, the moment when the original story, estranged from itself by images, by a new voice and a new tongue, begins its foreign adventure.

A Ritual Feat

"This was the universe about which we have read so much and never before felt: the universe as a clockwork of loose spheres flung at stupefying, unauthorized speeds."

—ANNIE DILLARD

ON FEBRUARY 26, 1979, the shadow of the moon passed over Greenland, parts of Canada, and the states of North Dakota, Washington, Oregon, Idaho, and Montana. Elsewhere in North America, the skies merely dimmed appreciably and portions of varying size—from nail clipping to rocker knife or *mezzaluna*—were seen (do not look directly!) to be excised from the solar disc. But at the pencil point where the moon's cone of darkness met the earth's surface, all went black. It was the last total eclipse to be seen in the United States in the twentieth century, and TV anchormen counted the hours, minutes, and seconds to totality as if awaiting a moon-shot or election result. A certain portentousness entered their language: an ABC announcer spoke of the "ritual feat" by which crowds sought the best vantage points, and addressed himself to viewers of the next total eclipse visible in the United States, on August 21, 2017: "May the shadow of the moon fall on a world in peace."

Annie Dillard published her essay "Total Eclipse" in the Spring/Summer 1982 issue of the literary quarterly *Antaeus*, and again later that year in her book *Teaching a Stone to Talk*. "It had been like dying, that sliding down the mountain pass" —the piece begins with the first of several descents, the first inkling that looking at the spectacle in the sky might also demand a glimpse within, a journey down "into the region of dread." The writer and her husband, Gary, are in a hotel near Yakima, Washington, and some unease about the very act of seeing is already in the air. Dillard lies in bed and tries not to look at a picture on the hotel-room wall: "It was a print of a detailed and lifelike painting of a smiling clown's head, made out of vegetables." In the two years that have passed between the eclipse and the writing of the essay, Dillard has forgotten many things, but not it seems this face, this Arcimboldo *manqué*, "or its lunatic setting in the old hotel."

The question is, in "Total Eclipse": Does Dillard know what she's looking at? A gulf opens, long before the moment of totality, between seeing and understanding: a void into which the author is pitched and must come up clutching—what? Images that might be real or might be metaphors, pictures composed of odd comparisons, efforts in prose not to end up missing the event, botching its description and placing on the page the written equivalent of a clown face made of vegetables. Attaining the top of a hill from which she'll view the eclipse, Dillard remarks that the valley below looks "like a thickness or sediment at the bottom of the sky." The air darkens without warning, like a race with no starter gun. The grass on the hill turns to platinum. The scene starts to resemble a photograph from the nineteenth century. Gary is in the photograph, and he seems to be speeding away, "down a chute of time." The moon heaves into position—"It did not look like the moon. It was enormous and black." People start to scream.

The sentence comes later, following totality and the shining miracle of an accompanying corona, in the aftermath of those deathly seconds, when the stone has been rolled away again. Everybody leaves quickly. Dillard and her husband find a restaurant full of other watchers, where they come back to life and start straight away to forget what they have just seen: after all, the "clamouring mind will hush if you give it an egg." Dillard struggles to recall the screaming and the speed of it all. Then the sentence: "This was the universe about which we have read so much and never before felt: the universe as a clockwork of loose spheres flung at stupefying, unauthorized speeds." There are small oddities and excellences of technique to admire in this sentence. The absence of a comma after "universe," which half implies there might be another one. The slight shift of tense, from "this was" to "have read." The combination of "stupefying" and "unauthorized," as if the universe were some ramshackle fairground ride that a delinquent carny boy has set going full pelt while his boss is not looking. The sentence, with its central colon, feels balanced but loose, centrifugal and strange.

But the sentence's more exacting thrills are in the nature of the image that it asks us to conjure. All along Dillard has had trouble seeing, but really *seeing*, the landscape and the appalling event—"appalling," that is, in the sense of casting a pall, shrouding itself at the moment it actually happens. It's the eye as much as mind that is "stupefied." She has to force herself—she who has hardly any knowledge of or feeling for physics, so she says—to picture otherwise what is going on: the music of the spheres gone manically out of tune, the stately orrery of the solar system running ragged. "How could anything moving so fast not crash, not veer from its orbit amok like a car out of control on a turn?" This amazing sight—just once in most lifetimes, so the ABC man says—is also a demand, or a test, as if an importuning divine voice had started up in the moment of totality: *Put your paltry language to work on* this*, mortal.*

To the alert and troubled essayist, a total eclipse is both a descriptive challenge and an opportunity to point, in description itself, to the limits of description: the lapses and pratfalls to which the writer's figural powers may succumb. (Anne Carson, in an essay on eclipses: "totality is a phenomenon that can flip one's ratios inside out.") In "The Sun and the Fish," her 1928 essay on viewing an eclipse in Yorkshire, Virginia Woolf prefaces the main event with a passage about her own variable facility for making word and image match in the mind. "When one says Queen Victoria, one draws up the most heterogeneous collection of objects, which it will take a week at least to sort." But when she says "Mont Blanc" or "Taj Mahal"—nothing, her mind is blank. Images marry emotions, and hope to thrive, but sometimes they do not. "Let us see that strange spectacle again"—the eclipse promises much when recalled by the writer. And sure enough, the images and metaphors proliferate: the sun is defeated in a race with the moon, the eclipse is like "the heeling over of a boat," the earth is skeletal and dead: "It hung beneath us, like a cage, like a hoop, like a globe of glass." But these images are swiftly overtaken by the memory of lizards and fish at London Zoo, and the way a bubble rises in an aquarium: "The silver drop bores its way up a spiral staircase."

What if Dillard's sentence is also a reflection on descriptive and figural language, on the fragile machinery of words and sentences and paragraphs, on the adventures (and consolations) this equipment makes possible? Early on in "Total Eclipse," she notes the presence in the hotel lobby of an aquarium with one large fish, and nearby a canary in its cage: "Beneath the cage, among spilled millet seeds on the carpet, were a decorated child's sand bucket and matching sand shovel." The bucket and shovel return, following the eclipse, when Dillard is sitting in the restaurant and hears a college student exclaim of the corona: "Did you see that little white ring? It looked like a Life

Saver. It looked like a Life Saver up in the Sky." And so it did, says Dillard. The young man has retained a power of image-making, however modest, that the essayist has temporarily lost. "The mind—the culture—has two little tools, grammar and lexicon: a decorated sand bucket and a matching shovel. With these we bluster about the continents and do all the world's work. With these we try to save our very lives."

In the hotel lobby too, at six in the morning, are six bald old men stupefied in front of the television. Most of them are awake, but it seems they might miss the eclipse:

> You might drown in your own spittle, God knows, at any time; you might wake up dead in a small hotel, a cabbage head watching TV while snows pile up in the passes, watching TV while the chili peppers smile and the moon passes over the sun and nothing changes and nothing is learned because you have lost your bucket and shovel and no longer care.

It's not clear to Dillard, who has come with the tools (or are they just a child's toys?) of word and syntax, that she will fare any better than these men when it comes to capturing the miracle. But in the meantime, it is hard not to see that they are part of the sentence too, that they compose their own lazy little universe, that their hairless old heads are loose spheres orbiting the vacancy of the TV, hoping some image will resolve itself.

Broken Tongue

"All dim, gently, slowly until in the dark, the absolute darkness the shadows fade."

—THERESA HAK KYUNG CHA

THE KOREAN-AMERICAN ARTIST AND WRITER Theresa Hak Kyung Cha published her book *Dictée* towards the end of October 1982. A week later she was raped and murdered in New York City. Hard not to think of *Dictée*, with its delicate, furious mix of autobiography, history, myth and avant-garde adventure with the page as a summation of Cha's work in image and word. And as a tragically punctual text about misogyny, religion, colonialism and capital. The book is at once intimate and erudite, organized around the lives and images of her own mother (born in China to an exiled Korean family), the early-twentieth-century Korean revolutionary Yu Guan Soon, the Greek Muses, Joan of Arc and Cha herself. *Dictée* is a novel, an essay, a prose poem—and a daring reflection on what it means to inhabit a language, or be denied a home there.

Like her mother, like Joan of Arc (a woman visited by voices), Cha lives between languages: English, Korean, the French she had studied and the Greek names that title her chapters: Clio, Calliope, Urania, Melpomene, Erato, Thalia, Terpsichore and Polyhymnia. (For the ninth Muse, Euterpe, who is associated with music, Cha substituted one of her own invention, a Muse of lyric poetry called Elitere.) In some of these chapters, or sections inside them, Cha writes a precise and conventional prose—for example, when she describes her mother's linguistic predicament:

> Mother, you are a child still. At eighteen. More of a child since you are always ill. They have sheltered you from life. Still, you speak the tongue the mandatory language like the others. It is not your own. Even if it is not you know you must. You are Bi-lingual. You are Tri-lingual. The tongue that is forbidden is your own mother tongue. You speak in the dark. In the secret. The one that is yours. Your own. You speak very softly, you speak in a whisper. In the dark, in secret.

Elsewhere, Cha writes in a variety of fractured styles, speaks a "broken tongue" that more urgently expresses the condition of being between, of trying to reproduce a speech dictated (in all its senses) for you, to you, despite you. As in this passage, which appears in both English and French:

Little at a time. The commas. The periods.
The pauses.
Before and after. Throughout. All advent.
All following.
Sentences.
Paragraphs. Silent. A little nearer. Nearer.
Pages and pages
in movement
line after
line
void to the left void to the right, void the
words the silences.

"All dim, gently, slowly until in the dark, the absolute darkness
the shadows fade." The sentence comes from a short, enigmatic
section of *Dictée* that seems to describe the experience (whose?
Cha's? her mother's?) of a darkened theatre or cinema. The
chapter is titled "Melpomene: Tragedy." It comes halfway
through the book and is still concerned with Cha's mother, with
the family's life in America and with the legacy of the Korean
War. (Cha was born in Busan during the war, and the family
moved to the US in the early 1960s.) This strange opening section of the chapter—one page, four short paragraphs—appears
on the righthand page, opposite a map of Korea, North and
South, bisected by the DMZ. Here is the opening paragraph:

179

She could be seen sitting in the first few rows. She would be sitting in the first few rows. Closer the better. The more. Better to eliminate presences of others surrounding better view away from that which is left behind far away back behind more for closer view more and more face to face until nothing else sees only this view singular. All dim, gently, slowly until in the dark, the absolute darkness the shadows fade.

Why this sentence and not another? Is it because it reminds me so much of certain sentences in Beckett? "A voice comes to one in the dark. Imagine. To one on his back in the dark." "But under us all moved, and moved us, gently, up and down, and from side to side." Beckett was certainly one of the teeming reference points Cha had in mind when she wrote *Dictée*. You can hear him in the verb-avoiding rhythms of the sentence, in its consoling repetitions of sound and word. But Beckett's is just one voice among many, some of which are Cha's and some not. (Stéphane Mallarmé was another early interest: the influence of his itinerant typography is visible in Cha's diverse arrangements of her text, and her taste for white space.) The sentence tends towards unity, sonically and semantically, all shadowy distinctions dissolving in the general dark. But like Beckett—only more so, because with her it is not a matter of elective exile and affinity—Cha writes from a place where no tongue is truly her own, but must be claimed and reclaimed, made and broken, renovated and abandoned to prove she was there.

One thing I notice late, before letting the sentence go: the way some expected commas fail to appear—a more conventional writer might like one after "slowly," and would definitely want one after "darkness"—until everything is sliding and obscure.

Saving Imprecision

"A slight sense of quotation marks hovers in the air but it is very slight—it may not even be there—and it doesn't dispel the atmosphere of dead-serious connoisseurship by which the room is dominated."

—JANET MALCOLM

IN 1994, JANET MALCOLM PUBLISHED IN *The New Yorker* a profile of the American painter David Salle, whose art of hectic juxtaposition and multifarious reference placed him blithely in the camp of postmodernism. The piece is titled "Forty-One False Starts," and purports to be exactly that: a series of opening passages, of varying lengths and modes of address, for an essay that remains—to use Marcel Duchamp's phrase—definitively unfinished. Or does it? In spite of Malcolm's performing a fragmentary, self-aware and therefore somewhat postmodern (or "postmodern") attitude to her subject and his work, "Forty-One False Starts" is also for better or worse a classic *New Yorker* profile, which does all the things that such an article is meant to do and, because this is Janet

Malcolm, something unsettlingly else too. We learn about Salle's background, the nature of his art and the nature of his success, what various art-world insiders make of the art and the success, about Salle's sense that the market and the critics have turned against him, the private self-doubt and public self-regard that come with such realizations. Drawing on many months, in fact years, of research and interviews, Malcolm arraigns Salle (if that is indeed what she does) as much by the atmosphere around him as what he says and the work he makes.

Malcolm is a prose master of coolly significant scene-setting. This is how she begins the first of her forty-one mini-essays on Salle; the writer is approaching the artist's studio:

> There are places in New York where the city's anarchic, unaccommodating spirit, its fundamental irrepressible aimlessness and heedlessness have found especially firm footholds. Certain transfers between subway lines, passageways of almost transcendent sordidness; certain sites of torn-down buildings where parking lots have silently sprung up like fungi; certain intersections created by illogical confluences of streets—these express with particular force the city's penchant for the provisional and its resistance to permanence, order, closure.

Malcolm's own resistance to the same qualities involves her in an orgy of provisionality and tentativeness. (How uncertain those repetitions of "certain" end up making us feel.) Which hesitation by no means means—and this is really the trick, to put it too crudely, of the piece—that we do not swiftly get close to Salle himself. Here are the opening sentences of some of her false starts. "The artist David Salle and I are sitting at a round table in my apartment." "The artist David Salle and I met for the first time in the fall of 1991." "David Salle's art has an appearance of mysterious, almost preternatural originality, and yet nothing in it is new." "All during my encounter with the artist David Salle—he and I met for interviews in his studio, on White Street, over a period of two years—I was acutely conscious of his money."

Being acutely conscious, in ways that engage her readers and make us feel decidedly her inferior, is very much Malcolm's essayistic style and strength. A certain kind of exposure, without mercy, is what she has been celebrated for—although she is rueful about the role of recording her subjects' weaknesses: "Every journalist who is not too stupid or full of himself to notice what is going on knows that what he does is morally indefensible. He is a kind of confidence man, preying on people's vanity, ignorance or loneliness, gaining their trust and betraying them without remorse." That sentence, which opens her 1990 book *The Journalist and the Murderer*, is so frequently quoted as to have turned into a hampering cliché when it comes to understanding what Malcolm does as a writer. The other aspect that gets talked up or down is her tendency—whether writing about controversies among psychoanalysts, trials for murder or fraud, the literary afterlives of Plath and Hughes—to fix (or fixate) upon details of the locale in which her drama takes place. In a review of Malcolm's 1999 book *The Crime of Sheila McGough*, Joyce Carol Oates wrote: "Malcolm is gifted with, if not accursed by, the allegorist's imagination, to which nothing merely *is*, but can be interpreted in broad, ethical terms." With Malcolm, everything *means*—especially what seems insignificant, ordinary, simply part of the ground on which the action is to be painted.

There is for example the frieze of almost excessively significant dwelling places that she describes in a 1986 profile of Ingrid Sischy, who was then the young editor of *Artforum* magazine. "A Girl of the Zeitgeist" appeared over two issues of *The New Yorker*, giving Malcolm considerable scope to spend time with Sischy and to interview everyone around her. In the opening paragraphs, Malcolm turns up at the loft apartment of the art critic and theorist Rosalind Krauss, and marvels at the austerity on show, the conspicuous display of high-toned reticence amid well-chosen and expertly placed items: an owl-shaped Art Deco table clock, a mysterious black-and-white photograph of ocean water, a geometric arrangement of dark blue armchairs. "But perhaps even stronger than the room's aura of commanding originality is its sense of absences, its evocation of all the things that have been excluded, have been found wanting, have failed to capture the interest of Rosalind Krauss." By contrast, the apartment of artist and critic John

Coplans "has the look of a place inhabited by a man who no longer lives with a woman. There are ill-defined living and working areas … punctuated by untidy mounds of things on which a grey-striped cat perches proprietorially."

In "A Girl of the Zeitgeist," the quotation marks arrive deep in the account of Sischy's career and character, when Malcolm considers the first magazine cover that her subject oversaw as editor. Sischy chose to reproduce on the front of *Artforum* the inaugural, June 1942, cover of *VVV* magazine: a short-lived Surrealist journal published in New York with the involvement of Marcel Duchamp, André Breton and Max Ernst. The green cover, with diagrams collaged by Ernst, shows its age in stains and a conspicuous cigarette burn, and Malcolm notes "the sense of quotation marks that they would help impart to the notion of a cover about a cover." "The sense of quotation marks"—it denotes here, as in "Forty-One False Starts," a level of self-awareness that is very much of its historical moment. Almost a decade apart, the two pieces bracket the period not of postmodernism itself—a messy term with quite different (if overlapping) applications and timescales in art, literature, philosophy and architecture—but of its entry into the mainstream, the word's appearance as shorthand for tendencies towards irony, recursiveness, reflexivity in the arts and, to some degree, in life. "Quotation marks" is shorthand for a shorthand, a metonym for the mise en abyme.

In the David Salle essay, "the sense of quotation marks"

becomes "a slight sense of quotation marks." (Or rather, in the original *New Yorker* version, "quotation mark"—an error, or an eccentricity, that was corrected when Malcolm reprinted the piece in her book *Forty-One False Starts*.) What is this "sense," exactly? Where, how and by whom is it felt? Does it belong only to Malcolm herself? She has employed such phrasing all through her career; it's already there in the first thing she published in *The New Yorker*, in 1963. This is a poem titled "Thoughts on Living in a Shaker House," in which Malcolm regrets and admires the hard, close, peculiar existence of her predecessors in the house: "Our rueful sense of lives ill-spent/ Is, in the end, impertinent." Malcolm's *sense* is keenly felt and somehow evanescent or uncertain. In a 2016 profile of the Chinese classical pianist Yuja Wang, she visits the musician's New York apartment, with its Steinway grand piano and its state of disarray, the latter reminding Malcolm, when she glances into the bedroom, of a college dorm: "There may be a few stuffed animals on the bed or maybe only a sense of them—I am not sure because I was at the apartment only once."

"Or maybe only a sense of them"—is it that the impression easily dissolves, or that it is present only to a sensibility as quick and acute as Malcolm's? She is like some meteorological device, feeling the very atmosphere. (In a piece about the fashion designer Eileen Fisher: "Her features are delicate, and there is a certain fragility about her, an atmosphere of someone who needs protection.") And this sense, this atmosphere, this aura—well, "it may not even be there." We are meant to trust Malcolm when she claims the sensation, and trust her again when she casts doubt upon it. This is quite the pact between author and reader, and not everyone is willing to enter into it. When "A Girl of the Zeitgeist" appeared in the autumn of 1986, the writer and critic Gary Indiana published in *The Village Voice* a riposte titled "Janet Malcolm Gets It Wrong." Malcolm's relative (and admitted) ignorance of the world of contemporary art meant she had been credulous, Indiana claimed, in the face of her interviewees' status or domestic decor: "Malcolm's gaze sweeps over the surfaces of people, places, and things, calmly categorizing them according to the inner logic of an intractable bourgeoise."

I consider Malcolm instead the kind of writer who thinks of categories like "bourgeois" as somewhat tractable—at the very least requiring intimacy, analysis, detail, some specifics before she will pronounce judgement. And even then, things remain uncertain. That is, as Indiana also discerns, she borrows a great deal from fiction, and especially from the nineteenth-century realist novel, where a good deal of the drama may turn on the ability to work out character or class from certain physical details of person or surroundings. When made by characters in novels, such judgements tend to be mistaken, just as much so when the character is also the narrator. If anybody knows this, it is Janet Malcolm, for whom the great Russians of the nineteenth century are her formal and her moral guides—and the great Americans: Edith Wharton and Henry James. (In "A Girl of the Zeitgeist," she compares Sischy to James's Fleda Vetch and Milly Theale.) Even an omniscient narrator, a narrator who has spoken to everyone who will speak, who has hung around the studio and the parties and the neighbourhood for years, gathering her evidence, making her notes and her precise appraisals—even such a figure may be working with material that threatens to dissolve at her touch or fade beneath her gaze. *A sense of* tells us how close Malcolm has got to the heart of things, and how much she doubts the mystery of character is penetrable in the first place.

Surprised His Shoes

"Paper storage, fragments of delirium eaten away by dust."

—FLEUR JAEGGY

FOR A LONG TIME, I was allergic to sentences without main verbs. Sentence fragments, as they say. My distaste wasn't—this would be madness—for *minor sentences*, mere asides or exclamations. Not at all. I mean instead those sentences, well beyond a blurted word or phrase, that carry on verbless but might equally have been rewritten to include a main verb, or been subsumed into a fuller, more conventional sentence either side. Years ago, I used to grade undergraduate essays in English literature, a discipline you might hope would be less rigid; but time and again in the margins I'd find myself dutifully huffing at my students: "This is not a sentence." And even, happy hypocrite: "Not a sentence!" In time, I cured myself of this pointless antipathy. After all, some of my favourite writers were markedly fond of the unverbed sentence. Elizabeth Hardwick, for example: "In the hotel lobby, tired bandsmen, dark glasses, ashen sleeplessness, oppressive overcoats, their wives, blond and tired."

Here is an instance from the first of three short essays in the Swiss writer Fleur Jaeggy's very short book *These Possible Lives*. "Paper storage, fragments of delirium eaten away by dust." Jaeggy is describing the domestic and writing habits, late in life, of the Romantic essayist Thomas De Quincey, whose work she has also translated into Italian. In a scant sixteen pages, the author of *Confessions of an English Opium-Eater* (1821) travels from the nursery to his deathbed, where he makes "a gracious corpse." De Quincey's life doesn't exactly unfold in this brief span, but instead is telegraphed in a series of obscurely privileged instants, a frieze of images detailing physiognomy, education, love, illness, imagination, death. In the second essay, Jaeggy treats John Keats in the same fashion, and in the third Marcel Schwob, the decadent writer who (like Baudelaire) had translated De Quincey into French, and whose *Imaginary Lives* (1896) is one of the models for Jaeggy's weirdly curtailed and oblique biographical essays. In all three pieces, Jaeggy gives us a vivid report of her subject's deathbed scene: De Quincey fading away genially among his papers, Keats expiring in Italy, Schwob's face turning to burnished gold while "the room smoked of grief."

There is something distinct from economy and compression in these brief lives: a tone hard to capture without excessive quotation. Jaeggy's sentences pile up, one dark thing after another, as if connecting tissue has been excised.

> Thomas De Quincey became a visionary in 1791 when he was six years old. His older brother William was looking for a way to walk on the ceiling upside down like a fly. Richard, whom they called Pink, signed on to a whaling ship and was captured by pirates. The other siblings were depressives. Thomas leafed listlessly through the pages of *Aladdin and the Enchanted Lamp*.

Jaeggy proceeds by simple statements in the past tense; but instead of a story, one has the impression she is describing a static scene or picture, all present tense.

In a *New Yorker* review, Sheila Heti has called Jaeggy's sentences "hard and compact, more gem than flesh. Images appear as flashes, discontinuous, arresting, then gone." This is all true, but there are knots and grains inside these images, faults along which the sentence-crystal seems to fracture. This is Jaeggy's rendering of De Quincey aged seventeen and newly arrived in London, where he befriended a young prostitute: "Cloaked in a driver's mantle, some legal papers, and frost, Thomas surprised his shoes and went skating down the street, coasting to a stop on the corner of Oxford Street in front of his little friend Ann." Here, biographical précis—De Quincey had indeed been keeping himself warm with his landlord's legal papers—

contends with something else: a subtle accent or peculiarity of image and phrase that remains quite mysterious. *Cloaked in frost*? *Surprised his shoes*? Jaeggy's main verbs, and her adjectival or attributive verbs, start to do strange things. In our sentence too. "Eaten away by dust"—this is a flummoxing formulation, no? And an unusual one even by the standards of Jaeggy's eccentric image-making. Verbs in the De Quincey essay tend towards verticality—"Dreams of terrific grandeur settled on the nursery...Old age descended on the child." "Eaten away by dust" is of another tendency, eroding and even ravaging where we might have expected slow accretion.

The whole essay has been directing us towards a scene in which dust and books and manuscripts are piling up, fuel for the fires that constantly threaten the aged writer's rented rooms. The Scottish author James Hogg recalled visiting De Quincey in one such apartment in Edinburgh, where a narrow path meandered from the doorway, through snowy mountains of paper, to the place near the fireplace where he wrote, and now mostly lived. Here is how Jaeggy approaches the scene:

They generally thought of him as an incendiary. "Papa," one of his daughters said, "your hair is on fire." De Quincey smoothed away the sparks with a hand. He was sometimes overcome with sleepiness in his studio and nodded off, pulling the candles down with him. Ash reliefs adorned his manuscripts. When the flames got too high he'd run to block the

door, afraid someone would burst in and throw water on his
papers. He put out fires with his robe, or the rug—the thin
cleric wrapped his words in smoke, chains, captivity, bondage.
When invited to dinner, he promised attendance, holding
forth on the subject of the enchantments of punctuality. At
the appointed time, however, he was elsewhere. Perhaps he
was studying pages piled up like bales of hay in one of the many
shelters that he never remembered having rented. Paper storage, fragments of delirium eaten away by dust.

The passage oscillates between Jaeggy's terse paraphrase of
details lifted from the biographical record—"He put out fires
with his robe, or the rug"—and a stranger register that turns
those details into lurid abstraction: "the thin cleric wrapped
his words in smoke, chains, captivity, bondage." At such
moments, it's as if the mineral hardness of Jaeggy's prose has
gone up in flames. Fire and smoke and the threat of domestic
conflagration are recurring subjects in Jaeggy's writing. She is
the translator of De Quincey's *The Last Days of Immanuel
Kant*, which is itself in large part an unacknowledged translation of *Immanuel Kant in seinen letzten lebensjahren*, published in 1804 by Ehregott Wasianski, an intimate of the
philosopher. In De Quincey's version, we discover that the
declining Kant was subject to the same incendiary lapses as
De Quincey: "These unseasonable dozings exposed him to
another danger. He fell repeatedly, whilst reading, with his

head into the candles; a cotton nightcap which he wore was instantly in a blaze, and flaming about his head." And this scene puts me in mind of the death in 1973 of Jaeggy's friend Ingeborg Bachmann; the Austrian poet and novelist had fallen asleep while smoking in her Rome apartment, and set her nightgown on fire. In her short story "The Aseptic Room," Jaeggy recalls conversations the two writers had about old age. In the space of a single short paragraph, Jaeggy then violently contracts the uncertain future:

> Old age, she said, is horrible. It's all horrible, I'd tell her. With a kind of glee. I tried to convince her that it's all truly horrible (at that time our lives weren't bad at all) and I meant it. Then her eyes radiated happiness and years went by. Swift. Every day I went to Sant'Eugenio, the burn unit. Twice I entered a room that had to be kept aseptic.

Seen in this light, the sentence—"Paper storage, fragments of delirium eaten away by dust"—seems a brilliantly condensed image of the slow certainty of age and decay, but also the ever-present possibility of sudden horror, catastrophe. As the three subjects of *These Possible Lives* draw close to death, the laconic enumeration of deathbed (or near-deathbed) facts intensifies Jaeggy's already staccato style. On Keats: "Stretched out on his bed, he gazed up at the rose pattern in the blue ceiling tiles. His eyes grew glassy. He spoke for hours in a lucid delirium. He never lost his faculties." The occasional verbless sentence goes further in this direction, subtracting all action and abstracting from character, from actor and acted upon, a cold reserve of impersonality.

Except, except: I have been misreading the sentence all along—or rather, reading the wrong sentence. I've been relying—it is all I can do—on the English translation of *These Possible Lives*, by Minna Zallman Proctor. (When I say "been relying on," I mean "been wholly seduced by.") And it's only lately, many months after first reading Jaeggy on De Quincey, that I've even thought to turn here to the original Italian: "*Forse scrutava i fogli accatastati come balle di paglia in una delle numerose dimore che non ricordava di avere affittato, depositi cartacei, frammenti di deliri smangiati dalla polvere.*" My sentence, the sentence I love most in *These Possible Lives*, is a seamless part of the whole, not a fragment. "Paper storage" is a curious choice on the translator's part, because the phrase *depositi cartacei* (literally, paper deposits) suggests a kind of bureaucratic or legal deposition, an official amassing—and it refers to the things themselves, not to the action of their archiving or the space in which they're placed. The singular "paper storage" sounds as though it means the old man's habit of hoarding, or refers to the apartments, not their contents.

When I first read this passage, I thought that De Quincey's rented rooms might be themselves the "fragments of delirium." Or that the short sentence conjured instead (or at the same time) some phantasmagoric impressions from the failing mind of the opium-eater. And these ideas, images, reflections—*these* were eaten away by dust? No, this train of thought was all wrong. It must be the papers, yellowed by candlelight, that we are to imagine powdered and shadowed with dust: thus obscured, they start to look *eaten away*. And here is the problem with pursuing the image so far, with trying to treat it almost literally: it is, as Heti told us, a crystal. But the sentence—the translator's sentence, which is not quite Jaeggy's—has pulled so much into itself that we can see the faults or inclusions (as they say in mineralogy), much haphazardly preserved material. It may well be that this is the only way in prose today, in English prose at any rate, to recapture the capacious quality of a writing like De Quincey's. For if we were to rehearse his long, involved sentences, sentences that threaten always to forget themselves, to fall asleep on us like the dozing essayist himself, then we would do nothing but point to their antique distance from our own structures and tones. Whether by larger design or localized expedient, Minna Zallman Proctor has given us a version of Jaeggy's sentence that retains, because it so abruptly and enigmatically departs from, the visionary languor of her subject and his prose.

Before She Solidified

"If Diana is present now, it is in what flows and is mutable, what waxes and wanes, what cannot be fixed, measured, confined, is not time-bound and so renders anniversaries obsolete: and therefore, possibly, not dead at all, but slid into the Alma tunnel to re-emerge in the autumn of 1997, collar turned up, long feet like blades carving through the rain."

—Hilary Mantel

Of course it is the extravagant image at the end—end of the sentence, end of the essay—that I notice first, that leaves me staring at the screen, scrolling back a little, mouthing the whole thing aloud in wonder. (Also, image-searching the feet of Diana, Princess of Wales: for which feet, no surprise, there exists a certain erotic constituency.) A succession of dumb, literal questions comes to mind. Was it raining in Paris on the night of 30 August, when she died? Not so far as I can discover. Did she have long feet? Apparently so, if this punning headline is to be believed: "Secrets of princess's size 9½ tootsies show why she falls in love with heels." Did she care to pop a collar? In the 1980s, obviously; near the end of the decade, on an official visit to Hong Kong, she wore Catherine Walker's white-pearl-crusted "Elvis Dress," with its streamlined Vegas collar. None of this will explain the aptness or oddity of Hilary Mantel's phrase, which concludes "The Princess Myth," a piece the novelist wrote for the *Guardian* to mark the twentieth anniversary of Diana's death. Who or what is this being that is not only mythic but inspires such intense imagery and ripe phrasing?

Mantel has been reflecting on several transformations undergone by Diana: from privileged but unexceptional adolescent to gawped-at, anointed consort; from brittle media darling to panicked media victim, then sleek sad apologist for the lost ones left to perish near the summit of the British state. Most of all, her blessed translation from body to myth and back again. Diana as medieval Assumption, perhaps with her feet still visible as she vanishes into the clouds. In the language Mantel uses for these exaltations (and degradations), Diana is both flesh and abstraction, her story never a simple passage from one state to the next. Consider where the sentence locates, or liberates, its dead princess: "what flows and is mutable, what waxes and wanes, what cannot be fixed, measured, confined"—what is all of that, exactly? Her afterliving image? Or a force more diffuse and general, an energy unleashed at her death?

Something strange, dislocating, happens with the sentence's

medial colon: "and therefore, possibly, not dead at all"—it simply doesn't flow, grammatically speaking, from the first half of the sentence. Who or what is not dead? Diana, of course. Except, not quite. After the opening clause, she has vanished as subject of the sentence, been subsumed in all that mutability, in the *whatness* and the plain (it is not so plain) use of the verb *to be*. So that when she comes together again, condenses into a ghost, we could do with a steadying pronoun: "and therefore, possibly, *she is* not dead at all…" As it is, one is left a little flummoxed while Mantel abruptly alters her tense with "slid," and then gives us the amazing, physically precise picture of the living (or living-dead) princess, who has survived the underground ordeal that fate prepared for her and come out sharp and intrepid, as in one of those photos of her advancing, visored, across a minefield.

It's a vivid but confusing sentence, the culmination of an essay that is all about Diana's shuttling between icon or caricature and something more elemental, protean, weirder. She is, predictably, a character from a fairy tale, a bride captured and encastled, lost among the fragmenting mirrors of her new royal identity. She is like the white goddess described by Robert Graves—a shape-shifter, variously virgin, hag, witch, and weasel. In life, her transformative capacity (or was it only necessity?) was tested most spectacularly on the day of her wedding to Prince Charles. Mantel had already, in an essay for the *Lon-*

don Review of Books, considered the protean bodies of the British royal family. Here she is, in a sort of rehearsal for our sentence, recalling the moment in July 1981 that Diana stepped from her carriage at St Paul's Cathedral:

> An everyday sort of girl had been squashed into the coach, but a goddess came out. She didn't get out of the coach in any ordinary way: she hatched. The extraordinary dress came first, like a flow of liquid, like ectoplasm emerging from the orifices of a medium. It was a long moment before she solidified.

Like ectoplasm, it's true: there are press photographs of a face-less Diana, dwarfed by the occult confection of her gown.

Elsewhere in the *Guardian* essay, Mantel writes: "For some people, being dead is only a relative condition; they wreak more than the living do. After their first rigor, they reshape themselves, taking on a flexibility in public discourse." Among the things Diana turns into, in other words, is language itself. ("Death is a displaced name for a linguistic predicament," writes Paul de Man in "Autobiography as De-facement.") Mantel has a particular skill for describing this language, as well as inventing her own troubled version of it. In an essay on Madonna, published in the *London Review of Books* in 1992, she concludes: "For anyone who wishes to become an adjective, Madonna is an inspiration." Diana, however, is subject to no such verbal reduction; the more she was imprisoned in mythology and media, the more something of her seemed to escape, until she became pure image, figure, poetry. (Pure kitsch too, especially in death; but Mantel's entire brief seems to be to scrape away at the national sentiment around Diana until something harder shows through.)

Mantel, in the *LRB* again: "She went into the underpass to be reborn, but reborn this time without a physical body: the airy subject of a hundred thousand photographs, a flicker at the corner of the eye, a sigh on the breeze." It was in this essay that Mantel, to the pretended horror of British tabloid newspapers, referred to Kate Middleton as "a jointed doll on which certain rags are hung." Of course she did not mean the actual Kate, but the bony phantasm those very papers had helped create. In the same piece, Mantel recalls seeing the Queen at a Buckingham Palace function: "I am ashamed now to say it but I passed my eyes over her as a cannibal views his dinner, my gaze sharp enough to pick the meat off her bones." Which is precisely how one is *meant* to look at a monarch: as a real body to be picked clean of regal meaning, butchered neatly into two persons, one actual and one significant.

As a stylist, Mantel is extraordinarily good at the combination of intimacy and detachment such moments demand—and not only when coming across a venerable royal personage at a party. In 2010, she published an essay about a recent experience of surgery. She does not say what the operation was for, but attends, not without some Gothicism, to the grisly aftermath.

> Within a few days, the staff are tampering with my spiral binding when the whole wound splits open. Blood clots bubble up from inside me. Over the next hours, days, nurses speak to each other in swift acronyms, or else form sentences you might have heard in Haworth: 'Her lungs are filling up.'

It takes a special kind of attitude to the human body, including one's own, and to language, to detach from the wounded, plethoric, congested flesh and start to joke that your (linguistic) predicament is that of a dying Brontë. But this mode of attention, and with it a flamboyant creepiness of metaphor, is frequently to be found in Mantel's work. There is a short story titled "Comma" that recalls in adulthood the narrator's excursion to spy on another child, who is disabled or disfigured. In the protagonist's memory, or imagination, this child, the "comma" of the title, is physically attenuated and faceless: "We saw a blank, we saw a sphere, it was without feature, it was without meaning, and its flesh seemed to run from the bone." As with the final clause of our sentence, I'm unsure what this last image is supposed to mean—or rather, it summons an image but I cannot quite see it. And I'm not sure I wish to.

There are those who think that is not how a sentence should behave. Mantel, as she tells us in her memoir *Giving Up the*

Ghost, has even pretended to be one of these people, when she is asked for advice about writing:

> Plain words on plain paper. Remember what Orwell says, that good prose is like a windowpane. Concentrate on sharpening your memory and peeling your sensibility. Cut every page you write by at least one third. Stop constructing those piffling little similes of yours. Work out what it is you want to say. Then say it in the most direct and vigorous way you can. Eat meat. Drink blood. Give up your social life and don't think you can have friends. Rise in the quiet hours of the night and prick your fingertips, and use the blood for ink; that will cure you of persiflage!

Not only does Mantel never take her own advice—"Persiflage is my *nom de guerre*"—but she has not even followed it in this passage of stern counsel. Never mind the pricking of thumbs and drinking blood; at "peeling your sensibility" we're already inside Mantel's peculiar image-repertoire.

Let's hear the sentence again, the perfectly weighted parallelism of its first half, the curious grammar of the second—for the first time, I have started to hear "slid" as a past participle, as if she had been slid into the tunnel.

> If Diana is present now, it is in what flows and is mutable, what waxes and wanes, what cannot be fixed, measured, confined,

is not time-bound and so renders anniversaries obsolete: and therefore, possibly, not dead at all, but slid into the Alma tunnel to re-emerge in the autumn of 1997, collar turned up, long feet like blades carving through the rain.

Is that persiflage, or a strange kind of precision? Some readers thought they knew. Four months after "The Princess Myth" appeared, the London *Times* published a list of the "best literary quotes of 2017"—if we're being pedantic, by "quotes" they meant "quotations." The final sentence of Mantel's essay appeared under the heading "Top pseud." The use of the prefix "pseudo" as a noun, describing a fake, affected, or pretentious person, may be traced to the pages of the *Times* itself, in 1829. The derivative "pseud" seems first to have been used in the mid-1950s, by Richard Ingrams, future editor of the satirical magazine *Private Eye*, which popularized the usage with its fortnightly assemblage of offending quotations, "Pseud's Corner." It is probably not unfair to say that use of the word "pseud" now marks one out as a particular type of older English male: privately educated but intolerant of intellectuals, materially well off but distrustful of extravagance or novelty in art or literature. This includes metaphor. Mantel's sentence marks her out, despite her prizewinning historical fiction, and regardless of her elevation to Dame Commander of the British Empire in 2015, as *not one of us.*

A brief coda concerning the contemporary fate of a

sentence. "The Princess Myth" appeared in the *Guardian* on Saturday, 26 August 2017. Like any article in a prominent newspaper, it was swiftly republished by news-aggregating websites. On the 28th, one such site, so I discovered in the course of research, posted a brutally garbled version of the essay, all of its syntax and punctuation intact, but word choices randomly botched with bad synonyms. Thus:

> If Diana is present now, it is in what floods and is mutable, what waxes and decreases, what cannot to be all right, quantified, detained, is not time-bound and so yields anniversaries antiquated: and therefore, maybe, not dead at all, but slithered into the Alma tunnel to re-emerge in the autumn of 1997, collar turned up, long feet like blades engraving through the torrent.

Here is Mantel's sentence defaced, become a pseudosentence, while its subject finally gives up her status as human child and takes to the waters and the wild—"slithered"—where she carves, engraves, *writes* herself at last.

Gusto Notwithstanding

"They'll probably rock up with hash and breadsticks, and quite possibly a dim jar of drilled out green olives, and people who stay late will horse into the breadsticks and the following day there'll be shards of breadstick all over the floor, ground to a powder in places, where people have stood on the bigger shards while talking to people they don't usually talk to, or even when dancing about perhaps."

—CLAIRE-LOUISE BENNETT

THE ENGLISH WRITER CLAIRE-LOUISE BENNETT, who has lived in the west of Ireland for many years, spent some of that time working in theatre. When asked about the relationship between the stage and her strikingly soliloquizing fiction, Bennett will say she quit the theatre in part so that she would not have to listen to so many competing voices, so that in fact she might escape from human beings entirely, and listen instead to the voices—how hard it is not to anthropomorphize—of things, places, atmospheres. Her stories and essays are about such solitude, among other matters. And yet, or maybe as a result, they feel, or sound, much more thoroughly *voiced* than most fiction you will read today; Bennett's protagonist, if that's what she is, sounds like she belongs to the unwilling community of Annie Dillard's "crank narrators." Related: when a friend told me I must read Bennett's short-story collection *Pond*, he said she had produced a fiction that was "all sensibility," and very nearly nothing else.

What happens to such a fictional voice when it, or its inventor, is asked to perform in public? I've heard people who've attended her appearances describe Bennett, and her style of reading, as "theatrical," and I can see (hear, that is) what they mean. There are points of italicized insistence, even violence, and moments when she seems to withdraw, throwing words or even whole sentences away *sotto voce*. She has the cadences of an actor, you might conclude. Except: what kind of actor speeds up and slows down in her delivery with, apparently, so little regard for sense? I've heard Bennett do it several times now, a mode of address that is by turns hectic and hardly there. It happens, for instance, in a reading I've just watched online, when she is reciting the story from which this sentence derives—she stops just before the paragraph that contains it. The effect here seems calculated, ideal, because "Finishing Touch" is a story all about presence and abeyance, a rush towards visionary certainty and retreat into—what? It's about getting carried away with yourself, and not getting carried away. Maybe.

The sentence in question concerns guests, and what if anything, in the way of food and drink, they can be asked to bring to the party. There are those who have definite culinary interests, or fixed tastes, that the narrator has already observed, and so can ask them to supply, as it were, the usual. "And, naturally, there'll be one or two you let off simply because, gusto notwithstanding, they've never demonstrated any discriminating interest in what they eat." Now will these individuals present and comport themselves, at the party? Our sentence wants to know.

At one level, that of its adverbs, the sentence stages very clearly its own contingency. Everything about the forthcoming party is uncertain: note the presence of "probably," "possibly" and "perhaps," as well as their alliterative affinity. What a clear sense Bennett's nameless narrator gives us of an event that is at the same time all up in the air. The sentence seems to grow more precise and assured as it progresses—but then there is the final "perhaps," undoing it all again. And isn't this oscillation between the exactingly exact and the falling-to-bits vague—isn't this all rather like the shape or structure or the very point of a party? Everything precisely arranged so that it may come pleasingly apart, all the guests (words? phrases?) feeling at home and adventurous at the same time? They are fragile things, parties.

Slow down, back up. The sentence comes from one of twenty stories, some of which are extremely short and oblique, and in these ways, as well as in their humour, remind me of the stories of Lydia Davis. Others in *Pond* are novel or strange in their syntax or vocabulary, to the extent that certain readers will call them "experimental." Most of the stories—they all seem to share this same narrator—concern a woman living in near-solitude in a cottage in what must be the west of Ireland. You could say next to nothing "happens" in these stories, except what never stops happening is her intense, funny, terrifying attention to the limited (or is it?) world she inhabits. She is obsessed, no, possessed, by things near at hand in her cottage, by containers, implements, furnishings and fixtures, none of which will quite remain how or where she wants them. The produce with which she returns from her forays to the nearest town comes together in an aesthetically consoling but impermanent array.

> Aubergine, squash, asparagus and small vine tomatoes look terribly swish together and it's no surprise at all that anyone would experience a sudden urge at any time during the day to sit down at once and attempt with a palette and brush to convey the exotic patina of such an irrepressible gathering of illustrious vegetables, there on the nice cool windowsill.

There are many "nice" things in the domesticated universe of *Pond*—"Some sort of black jam in the middle of porridge is very nice, very striking in fact"—"They are very nice to eat, oranges, when you've been having sex for ages"—and the word seems to denote an exquisite fragility or friability as much as it does something pleasant or precise.

Actually, Bennett's stories are full of such ordinary, even pitiful, words and phrases. "Actually" is one of them, and so is "even." Also "as a matter of fact" and "if you must know" and "for the simple reason that."* The effect is first of all to make the reader feel not only addressed but buttonholed, importuned, and likely to be here for a while, listening and possibly looking for a way out. Second, it's the narrator herself (like one of Beckett's) who is trapped by her own volubility, quite unable to stop. She runs on, like a sentence that has reached its logical terminus but then appended more matter, clause upon clause, without a care for its original cohesion. The narrator loses the run of herself (as one says in Ireland) as completely in the mode and degree of her attending to the world, as in her language, which unspools without end, knotted in itself by rhyme and repetition.

"I think I'm going to throw a little party. A perfectly arranged but low-key soirée. I have so many glasses after all. And it is so nice in here, after all." The opening sentences of

---

*I had an aunt, my father's sister, a garrulous unhappy person, who would frequently say, instead of "for the simple reason that" (but with the same grammatical intent) "for the simple reason is . . ." So, faced for example with the opportunity of a pleasant or diverting journey, she might say she could not go "for the simple reason is I'm not well." Sometimes she left a pause, the length of a comma, after the "is," and the formulation sounded less like a solecism. ("For the simple reason is, he's a bastard.") And on occasion she let the phrase hang in the air, as if all the simple reasons had escaped her.

"Finishing Touch" do some of the things I've been describing. Here is the narrator's anxiety, her devotion to things, her addiction to certain banal phrases ("after all") and their close repetition. Reflections follow on her motivation for hosting a party in the first place (it is because of the summer, she decides), on who to invite and who conspicuously not, and on where the guests will install themselves in her cramped home. There is the problem of her ottoman and who will sit on it; she hopes it will be a particular female friend. In fact, she has a great deal of detail about the party already in mind, more or less clearly. She wonders how things would go with her ottoman, if she were instead a guest at her own gathering:

> But I suppose I'd arrive a little later on and somebody else would already be sitting upon the ottoman very comfortably, holding a full glass most likely and talking to someone standing up, someone also holding a full glass of wine, and so I would stand with my fingertips upright on a table perhaps, which wouldn't be so bad, and, anyway, people move about, but, all the same, I would not wish to make it very plain just how much I'd like to sit there, on the ottoman—I certainly wouldn't make a beeline for it!—no, I'd have to dawdle in and perch upon any number of places before I'd dare go near it, so that, when finally I did come to sit on the ottoman, it would appear perfectly natural, just as if I'd ended up there with no effort or design at all.

Our sentence is neither as elaborately headlong nor as imaginative as this one; instead it's shorter, more sober, less emotionally fraught. And yet, what risks it takes: with the ordinary unguessable future that is a summer party; with its repetitions of sound and sense, strung out like fairy lights (if one fails the whole thing's a dud); with its colourful diction and at times opaque semantics; with its falling final clause. How many clauses? Six at my last count, or is it seven because one expects a comma before "and the following day"? It is one of the things I admire in Bennett, her ability to forgo commas when it suits her, and this in a prose that is generally so comma-ridden, built out of clauses, many of them very small, both hierarchical and—what is the word—not only serial but somehow *seasonal*. The lack of a comma is one of the ways she achieves a sense of slippage, getting carried away. Other tricks in that line, devices timed to that end: the almost rhymed contractions, "they'll" and "there'll," which pairing announces a shift undone again later, from probability to deep uncertainty about how things will go.

Bennett is a very nice maker of phrases—she's a reminder that "phrase-maker" ought to be an admiring term of art, not an insult reserved for writers who are judged insufficiently robust, altogether too transported by language. What have we got but our phrases, piling up? *Pond* is full of admirable examples (italics mine): "all sorts of *spread-eagled leaves* basking in oil and vinegar," or "I was feeling particularly *magnanimous and lithe.*" A few things strike me peculiarly in the sentence at issue. The "dim jar of drilled out green olives," for one thing: the mild affinity of "dim" and "drilled" of course—why no hyphen in "drilled out"?—but also the tart image conjured of an inadequate gift. And to think of the olives as having been drilled through, end to end! Like the big jade beads of a necklace. And the dimness of the jar, like stagnant green pond water.

It's about time I talked about "horse into." It is obvious what it means; you can probably well imagine the drunken or stoned chomping that's involved, but I still for the life of me cannot quite work out how or why it means what it means, idiomatically speaking. "Horse into" is not a phrase the OED recognizes, though you will find there several athletic or muscular uses of the verb "to horse." It can mean to drag: horsing over, rather than into. Or to drag oneself. ("Haul it over, haul it over," says Katharine Hepburn in *Bringing Up Baby*, passing herself off as a gangster's moll, Swingin' Door Susie. She might have said "horse it over"—same sense. In Ireland you'd also "hare over," a springier idiom.) It can mean to hoist, which might be the result of some historical mishearing. And there is horsing around: the sort of boisterous foalish behaviour that used to make my father say: "stop that horseplay." I have never heard or read "horse into," but it makes perfect sense.

I have just noticed—slow reader, slow thinker—the curious temporal-syntactic flow of the sentence. One thing follows another, crudely conjoined by "and." The first instance, "hash and breadsticks," hardly matters. It's the second, "and quite possibly," that gets us going, for a time, on what seems a seamless and plausible narrative path: "and quite possibly a dim jar of drilled out green olives, and people who stay late will horse into the breadsticks and the following day there'll be shards of breadstick all over the floor…" Except that each "and" is an exclamation, not a statement of proximity or progress. "And" gets us to a place beyond likely partygoer behaviour, into a realm of pure conjecture and even fantasy. And from this dreamy vantage we look down at the details: broken breadsticks, desultory dancing.

Consider that final clause: "or even when dancing about perhaps." It is unlike Bennett to sound so beside the point. Here is the sentence's first "or"—no more "and's—which I take to signal an afterthought, not an intensification of the narrator's vision for the party. But why "even," when this belated and breadstick-crushing dancing hardly sounds like an extension of the adventure of the sentence? Perhaps this "even" is the very definition of the gratuitous, the party's, and the sentence's, vestigial organ—it's appendix! Something like the "even" of Marcel Duchamp's title, *The Bride Stripped Bare by her Bachelors, Even*. But no—the role of deliberately deadening adjunct is surely trusted to the "about" in "dancing about." What is the difference between dancing and dancing about, if not that the second is the sort of thing you'd do very late and perhaps a little stoned at a party in a small cottage some way out of town when you know the host well enough to be invited but neither you nor she cares enough to ensure you've brought something delicious to eat or drink. "Or even when dancing about perhaps"—it sounds like an addendum, to the sentence and the party. A weak enough ending, after which it's time to quit and call it a night. Was my friend's word—"sensibility"—the right one for the reflective intensities of Bennett's strange narrator? Old-fashioned word, but how else to describe this fog of feelings, attachments and fantasies that she has become, and expresses so precisely yet so enigmatically in her prose?

Or Some Not-Stupid Sentences

"At any rate, there is a rolling, all-pervasive upwash of dread, one great, hot, shooting surge of dread-sensation through mind and body, a sense—perhaps?—of Time, carrying a body from Sunday night to Monday morning, to every Monday morning after that, and on and on, willy-nilly, to extinction, a mountainload of moments forcing the body from now to then, from drab to drab, from exposure to exposure, this progress, this exasperating, non-negotiable, obliterating motion forward into the dark—the dark what?"

—ANNE CARSON

IN THIS FICTION (a genre the poet does not usually admit to) titled "Flaubert Again," Anne Carson is writing about a writer who is trying to write, and so thinking about Flaubert, whose struggle with his prose was constant and painful, involving hours of dull agony upon the couch for every racking adventure with the sentence. And we feel here, in Carson's amazing lines, which are first of all about her narrator's reluctance to take a bath, on account of childhood memories of anxious Sunday nights, we feel the fear that comes with composing sentences and forcing them into the void. (Emerson, in his journal, in 1834: "The maker of a sentence, like the other artist, launches out into the infinite and builds a road into chaos and old Night, and is followed by those who hear him with something of wild, creative delight.")

What a trick that is at the end, as if the sentence itself is the onrush of dread, and the speaker has finally (but for how long?) managed to halt her catastrophist monologue and step back, only then to mishear or misread her own sentence, taking a noun (dark) for an adjective (dark) and thus not interrupting herself at all but rather amplifying the fear. Unless of course, and it seems quite likely, this is one of those ironic Carson moments—I can hear the tone with which she might read it in public—when something like an archly authorial voice intervenes, sharper and hipper and more knowing, so that "the dark what?" signals not a doubling of dread but the self-preserving distance of self from self. I *think* that may be what's happening, but the truth is: I tried to take notes on this sentence, but all I came up with was this ambiguous doodle

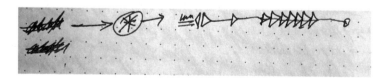

Like How If

"Inadmissible information is inadmissible because it provokes a kind of social discomfort, like how if a group of poor people are in the room with one not-poor person the poor people might without conferring about it work together to carefully conceal their own poverty for the benefit of the other, not-poor person, sometimes going so far as to increase their poverty by paying for the things they cannot afford."

—ANNE BOYER

THERE ARE SO MANY THINGS—IT is partly a book about things—to admire in Anne Boyer's book *Garments Against Women*, published in 2015. Some of these belong to the order of what one might once have called subject matter. Boyer is a poet who broaches an exhilarating range of ideas, experience, history, intimacies, abstractions and, as here, political realities. (Political realities have a habit of disguising themselves in, or as, matters of interpersonal protocol.) In *Garments Against Women* she writes about literature as preserve of the property-owning class; what it means to be well or happy in a society that demands and denies the conditions of wellness and happiness; the state of *not writing*, otherwise known as *life*; the rigours of making (especially clothes, also books) as possible, or impossible, affront to digital living; what it might mean to be a woman and a poet, of all things, in the rotten-empire stage of Capital. And she invokes many writers, including Rousseau, Baudelaire, Lautréamont, Artaud and Mary Wollstonecraft, who supplies an epigraph: "the events of her past life pressing on her, she resolved circumstantially to relate them, with the sentiments that experience, and more matured reason, would naturally suggest."

Garments Against Women is a collection of poems, an essay or essays, a memoir and (or) an argument. It has been described as a book of fragments, perhaps because that is the form we live in most urgently (or maybe most easily) today. Brevity, distraction, disjunction, aphorism, wit, montage, quotation, unfinishedness and ruination: these are meant to be our contemporary conditions and our favoured aesthetic reactions to our conditions. But there are fragments and fragments. Boyer's have an uncommon solidity; they are logical and unlyrical, sitting on the page more like monuments than fleeting *pensées*. She is a writer of *paragraphs*. (White space at either end, no tabs: a way of organizing matter on the page, or rather on the screen, that seems natural to us today, though it is no such thing.) Yes, of course, she has thought about Gertrude Stein and which is more emotional, a sentence or a paragraph. Sometimes, as in this sentence, the sentence is also a paragraph. Boyer's merciless logic demands, amid many short adjectives, adverbs and prepositions, much repetition of terms—"inadmissible," "information," "poor," "not-poor," "people," "poverty"—and I think it is this that impresses me most in the sentence. The repetitions are not like Stein's, which are all made for the ear, but possess a graphic force: this sentence (this paragraph) bristles with them. This is a kind of care, and a kind of fury.

Towards the end of *Garments Against Women*, Boyer recounts a narrative from Rousseau's *Émile*, later retold by Wollstonecraft in *A Vindication of the Rights of Woman*. Rousseau had known, he says, a little girl who, eager to learn to write before she could read, continually inscribed the letter *O* with a needle—no other letter, just a parade of *O*s. And then one day she caught a glimpse of herself in the mirror as she was writing and, finding herself awkward or ugly, promptly gave up her practice. According to Rousseau, the anecdote points to the natural vanity of women: a lesson Wollstonecraft dismisses as "ridiculous." Here is Boyer: "Rousseau believed the O's to be O's, but every O could have been, also, every letter and every word for the little girl: each O also an opening, a planet, a ring, a word, a query, a grammar. One O could be an eye, another a mouth, another a bruise, another a calculation." By a line of *O*s the girl might have meant: "I understand the proximate shape of the fountain." Or: "Apples are smaller than the sun." Or: "My mother." *O, o, o, o* was a revolutionary code, and when she put down her pen it was because she had already written what she needed to write.

Readings

James Baldwin, *Collected Essays* (New York: Library of America, 1998).

Whitney Balliett, *Collected Works: A Journal of Jazz 1954–2000* (New York: St. Martin's Press, 2000).

Roland Barthes, *Album: Unpublished Correspondence and Texts*, trans. Jody Gladding (New York: Columbia University Press, 2018).

———, *Empire of Signs*, trans. Richard Howard (New York: Hill and Wang, 1983).

———, *The Pleasure of the Text*, trans. Richard Miller (New York: Hill and Wang, 1975).

———, *Sade/Fourier/Loyola*, trans. Richard Miller (New York: Hill and Wang, 1976).

———, *S/Z*, trans. Richard Miller (New York: Farrar, Straus & Giroux, 1991).

Samuel Beckett, "The Capital of the Ruins," in Eoin O'Brien, *The Beckett Country* (London: Faber & Faber, 1986).

———, *The Complete Dramatic Works* (London: Faber & Faber, 1986).

———, *The Letters of Samuel Beckett*, Volume 2. 1941–1956, ed. George Craig et al. (Cambridge: Cambridge University Press, 2011).

Walter Benjamin, *The Arcades Project*, trans. Howard Eiland and Kevin McLaughlin (Cambridge, MA.: Harvard University Press, 1999).

Claire-Louise Bennett, *Pond* (Dublin: Stinging Fly, 2015).

Elizabeth Bowen, *A Time in Rome* (London: Vintage, 2003).

Anne Boyer, *Garments Against Women* (London: Penguin, 2019).

Maeve Brennan, *The Long-Winded Lady* (Dublin: Stinging Fly, 2017).

Charlotte Brontë, *Villette* (London: Penguin, 1979).

Sir Thomas Browne, *The Major Works*, ed. C. A. Patrides (London: Penguin, 1977).

Anne Carson, "Flaubert Again," *The New Yorker*, October 22, 2018.

———, *Short Talks* (London, Ontario: Brick Books, 1992).

Theresa Hak Kyung Cha, *Dictée* (Berkeley, CA: University of California Press, 2001).

Lydia Davis, *Essays One* (New York: Farrar, Straus & Giroux, 2019).

Thomas De Quincey, *Confessions of an English Opium-Eater* (London: Mac-Donald, 1956).

———, *The Works of Thomas De Quincey*, ed. Grevel Lindop (London: Pickering and Chatto, 2000–2003).

Joan Didion, *Telling Stories* (Berkeley, CA: The Friends of the Bancroft Library, 1978).

———, *The 1960s & 70s*, ed. David L. Ulin (New York: Library of America, 2019).

———, uncredited photograph captions, *Vogue* (US), August 1, 1965.

———, *The Year of Magical Thinking* (New York: Knopf, 2005).

Annie Dillard, *Teaching a Stone to Talk* (Edinburgh: Canongate, 2017).

John Donne, *Selected Prose* (London: Penguin, 1987).

George Eliot, *The Journals of George Eliot* (Cambridge: Cambridge University Press, 1998).

———, *Middlemarch* (London: Penguin, 1994).

Stanley Fish, *How to Write a Sentence: And How to Read One* (New York: Harper, 2011).

William H. Gass, *Habitations of the Word* (New York: Simon & Schuster, 1984).

Elizabeth Hardwick, "Billie Holiday," *The New York Review of Books*, March 4, 1976.

———, *The Collected Essays* (New York: New York Review Books, 2017).

———, *Sleepless Nights* (New York: New York Review Books, 2001).

Fleur Jaeggy, *These Possible Lives*, trans. Minna Zallman Proctor (New York: New Directions, 2017).

Wayne Koestenbaum, *Notes on Glaze* (New York: Cabinet Books, 2016).

Janet Malcolm, "Forty-One False Starts," *The New Yorker*, July 11, 1994.

——, *Forty-one False Starts* (New York: Farrar, Straus & Giroux, 2013).

——, *Nobody's Looking at You: Essays* (New York: Farrar, Straus & Giroux, 2019).

Hilary Mantel, *The Assassination of Margaret Thatcher: Stories* (London: Fourth Estate, 2015).

——, "Meeting the Devil," *London Review of Books*, Vol. 32, No. 21, November 4, 2010.

——, "Plain Girl's Revenge Made Flesh," *London Review of Books*, Vol. 14, No. 8, April 23, 1992.

——, "The Princess Myth," *The Guardian*, August 26, 2017.

——, "Royal Bodies," *London Review of Books*, Vol. 35, No. 4, February 21, 2013.

Joe Moran, *First You Write a Sentence* (London: Viking, 2018).

Frank O'Hara, *What's with Modern Art?*, ed. Bill Berkson (Austin, TX: Mike and Dale's Press, 1999).

Walter Pater, *The Renaissance: Studies in Art and Poetry* (London: Fontana, 1964).

John Ruskin, *Selected Writings* (Oxford: Oxford University Press, 2004).

——, "The Storm-Cloud of the Nineteenth Century," in *The Works of John Ruskin*, Vol. XXXIV, ed. E. T. Cook and A. Wedderburn (London: George Allen, 1908).

W. G. Sebald, *The Rings of Saturn*, trans. Michael Hulse (London: The Harvill Press, 1998).

Robert Smithson, *The Collected Writings*, ed. Jack Flam (Berkeley, CA: University of California Press, 1996).

Susan Sontag, *Debriefing: Collected Stories* (New York: Farrar, Straus & Giroux, 2017).

Gertrude Stein, *How to Write* (New York: Dover, 1975).

———, *Look at Me Now and Here I Am* (London: Penguin, 1990).

William Shakespeare, *Hamlet* (London: Bloomsbury, 2006).

Virginia Tufte, *Artful Sentences: Syntax as Style* (Cheshire, CT: Graphics Press, 2006).

Virginia Woolf, "On Being Ill," *The New Criterion*, January 1926.

———, *Selected Essays*, ed. David Bradshaw (Oxford: Oxford University Press, 2008).

Acknowledgments

SOME OF THESE ESSAYS—ON Hardwick, Donne, Woolf, Dillard, Mantel, Eliot, and Jaeggy—appeared first in *Cabinet* magazine; many thanks to the editor in chief Sina Najafi for his enthusiasm and rigour. The essay on Joan Didion was tested out as part of "The Virtual Sentence," an event at *Cabinet*'s space in Berlin, in January 2020; thanks to Jeff Dolven, Jan Mieszkowski, Sally O'Reilly, and Elena Vogman. A version of the short piece on Shakespeare was published in *Walker and Walker: Nowhere Without No(w)*, the catalogue of an exhibition at the Irish Museum of Modern Art in 2019.

Wayne Koestenbaum provoked me to write about the sentence by Claire-Louise Bennett; John Vaughan pointed me (back) towards Elizabeth Bowen; I had not even heard of Whitney Balliett until I read Sam Stephenson on him. I was introduced to the work of Theresa Hak Kyung Cha by Cathy Park Hong's book *Minor Feelings*. My students and colleagues at Queen Mary University of London and the Royal College of Art helped me figure out what I thought about many of the writers discussed here.

Huge thanks to Olivia Laing and Ian Patterson.

Thanks to my editors Jacques Testard and Susan Barba, and all at Fitzcarraldo Editions and New York Review Books. The book was also made possible by a generous grant from Arts Council England.

Emily LaBarge first suggested I write a book about sentences—her influence is on every page.

Errors and lapses are all my own.

BRIAN DILLON was born in Dublin in 1969. His books include *Essayism*, *The Great Explosion* (short-listed for the Ondaatje Prize), *Objects in This Mirror*, *I Am Sitting in a Room*, *Sanctuary*, *Tormented Hope: Nine Hypochondriac Lives* (short-listed for the Wellcome Book Prize), and *In the Dark Room*, which won the Irish Book Award for nonfiction. His writing has appeared in *The Guardian*, *The New York Times*, *London Review of Books*, *The Times Literary Supplement*, *Bookforum*, *frieze*, and *Artforum*. He is the UK editor of *Cabinet* magazine and teaches creative writing at Queen Mary University of London.